Noah

aliya

HOUGHTON MIFFLIN HARCOURT
SOUTH CAROLINA
JOURNEYS

Program Authors

James F. Baumann · David J. Chard · Jamal Cooks
J. David Cooper · Russell Gersten · Marjorie Lipson
Lesley Mandel Morrow · John J. Pikulski · Héctor H. Rivera
Mabel Rivera · Shane Templeton · Sheila W. Valencia
Catherine Valentino · MaryEllen Vogt

Consulting Author
Irene Fountas

Cover illustration by Bill Cigliano.

Printed in the United States of America

ISBN-13   978-0-547-48925-4

3 4 5 6 7 8 9 10 0914   19 18 17 16 15 14 13 12

4500362924   A B C D E F G

HOUGHTON MIFFLIN HARCOURT
School Publishers

Unit 4

Heroes and Helpers

Big Idea We can all make a difference.

Lesson 16

Vocabulary in Context. 10
Comprehension: Story Structure • Infer/Predict. 13

Mr. Tanen's Tie Trouble REALISTIC FICTION 14
written and illustrated by Maryann Cocca-Leffler

Your Turn. 35

Playground Fun! INFORMATIONAL TEXT 36
Making Connections 39
Grammar/Write to Express 40

Lesson 17

Vocabulary in Context. 44
Comprehension: Sequence of Events • Visualize 47

Luke Goes to Bat REALISTIC FICTION 48
written and illustrated by Rachel Isadora

Your Turn. 69

Jackie Robinson INFORMATIONAL TEXT 70
Making Connections 73
Grammar/Write to Express 74

Lesson 18

Vocabulary in Context. 78
Comprehension: Understanding Characters • Analyze/Evaluate . 81

My Name is Gabriela BIOGRAPHY 82
by Monica Brown • illustrated by John Parra

Your Turn. 101

Poems About Reading and Writing POETRY 102
Making Connections 105
Grammar/Write to Express 106

Lesson 19

Vocabulary in Context. 110
Comprehension: Text and Graphic Features • Question. 113

The Signmaker's Assistant HUMOROUS FICTION 114
written and illustrated by Tedd Arnold

Your Turn. 137

The Trouble with Signs PLAY 138
Making Connections 141
Grammar/Write to Express 142

Lesson 20

Vocabulary in Context. 146
Comprehension: Compare and Contrast • Monitor/Clarify . . . 149

Dex: The Heart of a Hero FANTASY. 150
by Caralyn Buehner • illustrated by Mark Buehner

Your Turn. 173

Heroes Then and Now INFORMATIONAL TEXT. 174
Making Connections 177
Grammar/Write to Express 178

Reading Power 182
Unit 4 Wrap-Up 184

Unit 5

Changes, Changes Everywhere

Big Idea Living things change over time.

Lesson 21

Vocabulary in Context. 186
Comprehension: Main Ideas and Details • Infer/Predict 189

Penguin Chick NARRATIVE NONFICTION 190
by Betty Tatham

Your Turn. 207

Animal Poems READERS' THEATER: POETRY. 208
Making Connections 211
Grammar/Write to Inform 212

Lesson 22

Vocabulary in Context. 216
Comprehension: Understanding Characters • Question. 219

Gloria Who Might Be My Best Friend
REALISTIC FICTION 220
by Ann Cameron • illustrated by Mike Reed

Your Turn. 237

How to Make a Kite INFORMATIONAL TEXT 238
Making Connections 241
Grammar/Write to Inform 242

4

Lesson 23

Vocabulary in Context 246

Comprehension: Conclusions • Summarize 249

The Goat in the Rug NARRATIVE NONFICTION 250

by Charles L. Blood and Martin Link • illustrated by Nancy Winslow Parker

Your Turn 269

Basket Weaving INFORMATIONAL TEXT 270

Making Connections 273

Grammar/Write to Inform 274

Lesson 24

Vocabulary in Context 278

Comprehension: Cause and Effect • Visualize 281

Half-Chicken FOLKTALE 282

by Alma Flor Ada • illustrated by Kim Howard

Your Turn 299

The Lion and the Mouse FABLE 300

Making Connections 303

Grammar/Write to Inform 304

Lesson 25

Vocabulary in Context 308

Comprehension: Sequence of Events • Monitor/Clarify 311

How Groundhog's Garden Grew FANTASY 312

written and illustrated by Lynne Cherry

Your Turn 333

Super Soil INFORMATIONAL TEXT 334

Making Connections 337

Grammar/Write to Inform 338

Reading Power 342

Unit 5 Wrap-Up 344

Unit 6

What a Surprise!

Big Idea A surprise can change your life.

Lesson 26

Vocabulary in Context	346
Comprehension: Story Structure • Infer/Predict	349
The Mysterious Tadpole FANTASY	350
written and illustrated by Steven Kellogg	
Your Turn	371
From Eggs to Frogs INFORMATIONAL TEXT	372
Making Connections	375
Grammar/Write to Respond	376

Lesson 27

Vocabulary in Context	380
Comprehension: Fact and Opinion • Question	383
The Dog That Dug for Dinosaurs BIOGRAPHY	384
by Shirley Raye Redmond • illustrated by Stacey Schuett	
Your Turn	401
La Brea Tar Pits INFORMATIONAL TEXT	402
Making Connections	405
Grammar/Write to Respond	406

Lesson 28

Vocabulary in Context. 410
Comprehension: Text and Graphic Features • Analyze/Evaluate 413

Working in Space INFORMATIONAL TEXT 414
by Patricia Whitehouse

Your Turn. 431

Space Poems POETRY 432
Making Connections 435
Grammar/Write to Respond 436

Lesson 29

Vocabulary in Context. 440
Comprehension: Understanding Characters • Summarize. . . . 443

Two of Everything FOLKTALE 444
written and illustrated by Lily Toy Hong

Your Turn. 461

Stone Soup READERS' THEATER TRADITIONAL TALE. 462
Making Connections 465
Grammar/Write to Respond 466

Lesson 30

Vocabulary in Context. 470
Comprehension: Compare and Contrast • Visualize 473

Now & Ben INFORMATIONAL TEXT 474
written and illustrated by Gene Barretta

Your Turn. 493

A Model Citizen INFORMATIONAL TEXT. 494
Making Connections 497
Grammar/Write to Respond 498

Reading Power 502
Unit 6 Wrap-Up 504
Glossary G1

Heroes
and Helpers

Unit 4

Big Idea

We can all make
a difference.

Paired Selections

Lesson 16

Mr. Tanen's Tie Trouble
Realistic Fiction
page 14

Playground Fun!
Informational Text: Science
page 36

Lesson 17

Luke Goes to Bat
Realistic Fiction
page 48

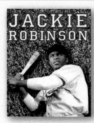

Jackie Robinson
Informational Text: Technology
page 70

Lesson 18

My Name is Gabriela
Biography: Social Studies
page 82

Poems About Reading and Writing
Poetry
page 102

Lesson 19

The Signmaker's Assistant
Humorous Fiction
page 114

The Trouble with Signs
Play
page 138

Lesson 20

Dex: The Heart of a Hero
Fantasy
page 150

Heroes Then and Now
Informational Text: Social Studies
page 174

Lesson 16

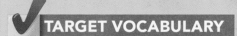
TARGET VOCABULARY

received

account

budget

disappointed

chuckled

staring

repeated

fund

Vocabulary
Reader

Context
Cards

Vocabulary in Context

- Read each Context Card.
- Use a Vocabulary word to tell about something you did.

1 received

The boys received some money for raking leaves in the yard.

2 account

The girl opened a bank account with the money from her allowance.

3 budget

A budget is a plan for how you should spend your money.

My budget for the Field Trip
I have $11.
I will spend $4 on lunch.
I will spend $5 on souvenirs.
I will spend $2 on a snack.

4 disappointed

He was disappointed, or sad, that he would not be able to buy the book.

5 chuckled

Her dad chuckled when he saw her tiny piggy bank.

6 staring

The girl was staring at the money. Should she save it or spend it?

7 repeated

The car wash was such a big success that the class repeated it in May.

8 fund

The players got new shirts by raising money for the team fund.

11

Background

Fundraisers Many schools raise money to help their budget. Everyone works hard at these events. People have chuckled at talent shows. They can be seen staring at delicious bake-sale food. No one is disappointed at a car wash.

When money is received, it goes into a bank account. The school uses this money to buy what it needs. If the fund runs low, the fundraising can be repeated.

A car wash is one way schools raise money for special things they need.

Comprehension

✔ TARGET SKILL **Story Structure**

In *Mr. Tanen's Tie Trouble,* Mr. Tanen thinks he has an easy solution, but he creates a new problem instead. In this story, is there a solution that makes everyone happy? As you read, look for events that are clues. Add them to a story map like this one.

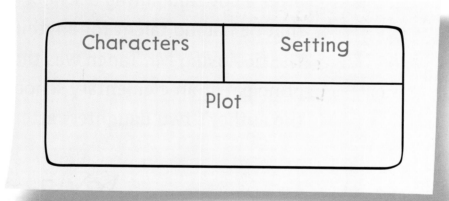

Characters	Setting
Plot	

✔ TARGET STRATEGY **Infer/Predict**

Use the information from your story map and what you already know to infer people's feelings in different parts of the story. Think about what you know to predict what will happen next. As you read, check to see if your predictions are correct.

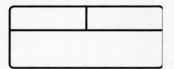

MEET THE AUTHOR AND ILLUSTRATOR

Maryann Cocca-Leffler

Many of Maryann Cocca-Leffler's books are based on her own life. *Clams All Year* is about the time she went clam digging with her grandpa following a big storm. She wrote *Jack's Talent* after a boy said during a school visit that he had no talent for anything. The tie-loving Mr. Tanen was the principal at an elementary school that the author's two daughters attended.

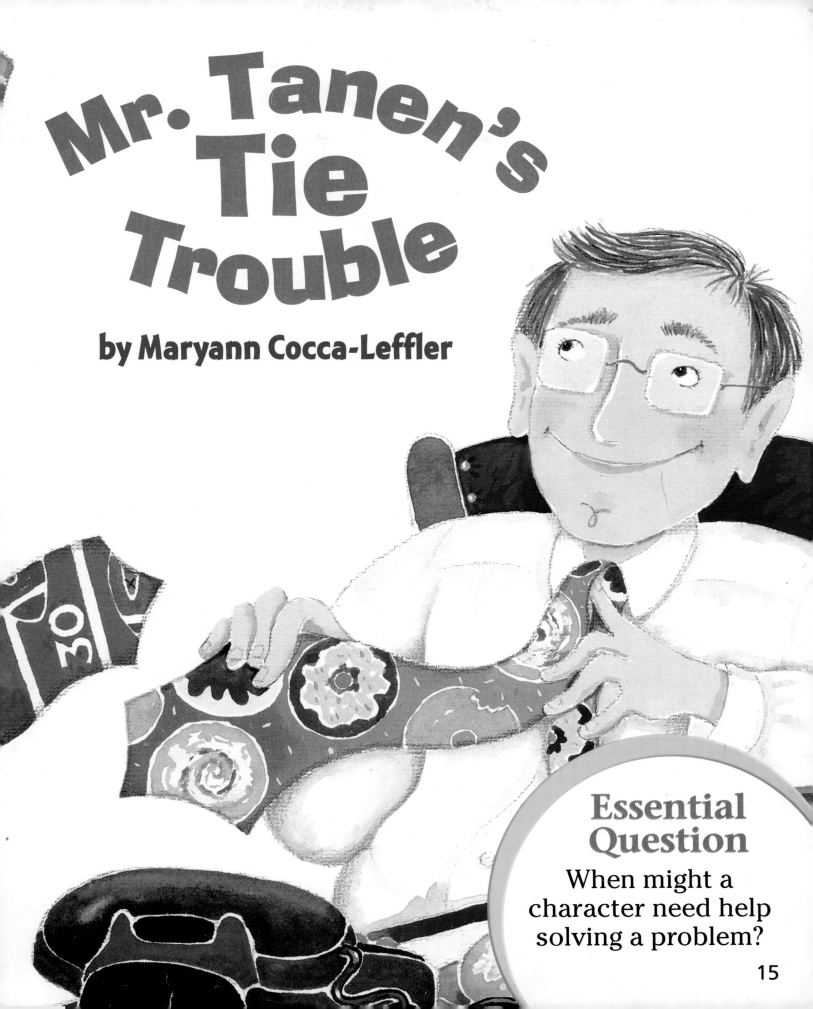

Mr. Tanen's Tie Trouble

by Maryann Cocca-Leffler

Essential Question

When might a character need help solving a problem?

Mr. Tanen loves being the principal of the Lynnhurst School. He also loves ties. In fact, he has almost one thousand crazy ties!

When Mr. Tanen returned from winter vacation, he received a call from Mr. Apple at the School Department. Mr. Apple told him that because many things at the school had to be fixed, there wasn't enough money left for a new playground.

Mr. Tanen sadly hung up the phone and gazed out at the broken-down playground. He heard a *clink-clank*. He looked up to see Kaylee and Alex lugging in a big jar filled with money.

"Here it is! $148.29 for the playground fund!" said Kaylee proudly.

"New playground, here we come!" cheered Alex.

Mr. Tanen didn't know what to say.

After school, Mr. Tanen sat in his office staring at the jar. He sighed. "Now I'm in a real pickle! This is not enough money for a playground. The kids will be so disappointed."

Mr. Apple's words floated around in his head:

"The playground will have to wait."

"You'll think of something."

"I wish our account was as full as your tie closet."

"Hmm . . . as full as my tie closet!" repeated Mr. Tanen.

STOP AND THINK
Author's Craft What does the author mean when she says that "words floated around in his head"?

18

He jumped up, opened his closet, and shouted, "That's IT! MY TIES! Lynnhurst School WILL have a new playground!"

The next day, the entire town was plastered with signs.

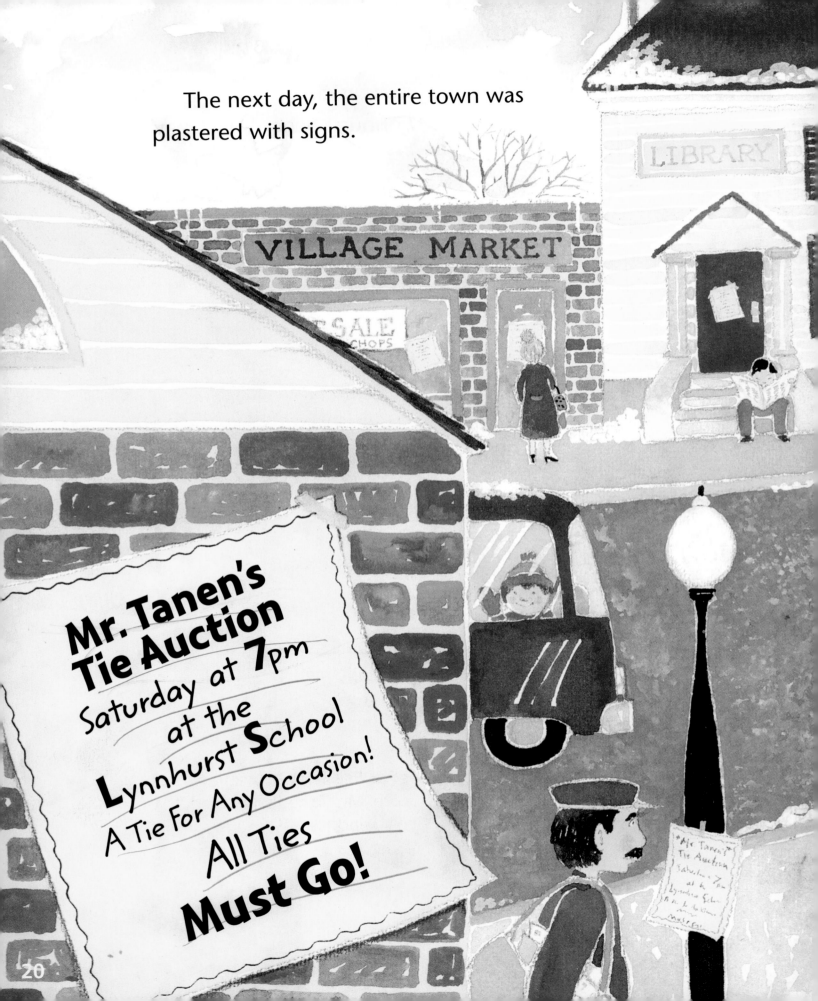

VILLAGE MARKET

LIBRARY

Mr. Tanen's Tie Auction
Saturday at 7pm
at the
Lynnhurst **S**chool
A Tie For Any Occasion!
All Ties
Must Go!

20

STOP AND THINK

Infer/Predict Will selling ties solve Mr. Tanen's problem? As you read, see if you are right.

21

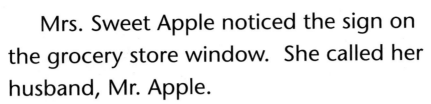

Mrs. Sweet Apple noticed the sign on the grocery store window. She called her husband, Mr. Apple.

"Why is Mr. Tanen selling all his ties? Has he gone crazy?"

Mr. Apple told her about the school budget and the playground money.

The town was buzzing all day . . .

Mrs. Sweet Apple called Monsieur Bijou at the bakery,

who called Cleo at the
cleaners,

who called Dr. Demi the
dentist . . .

It went on and on, until even
Zack, the night watchman at the
zoo, got the word:

"Mr. Tanen is selling his ties!"

On Saturday, the whole town showed up for the auction. Monsieur Bijou started the bidding. "I'll give you $50 for the Doughnut and Danish Tie!"

Lolly the librarian bought the Book Tie.

Dr. Demi was the proud owner of the Toothbrush Tie.

Kaylee handed over her entire piggy bank for the Hot Dog Tie.

Mrs. Sweet Apple just had to have the Wedding Bells Tie, and of course, Mr. Apple chuckled as he paid quite a bit of cash for the Crabapple Tie.

24

The auction was a huge success! Every tie was sold, except one. Mr. Tanen couldn't part with his beloved Blue Ribbon Tie. It was a present from Mr. Apple for being a great principal. He looked out at a sea of townspeople, all wearing his ties.

"Thank you all. I have always taught my students, 'The more you give, the more you get.' With this money, the Lynnhurst School will have a new playground!"

Mr. Tanen swallowed hard. "My ties now belong to the town. Wear them proudly."

STOP AND THINK

Story Structure How does the auction solve Mr. Tanen's problem? What new problem might it create?

And throughout the spring, that's just what everyone did.

But sometimes Mr. Tanen would forget his closet was empty. He would open it to get a tie, and with a tinge of sadness, he would remember. He only had one tie—and he was wearing it. Then he'd look outside at the playground being built.

"You have to give to get," he thought.

Soon it was Opening Day at the new playground. Mr. Tanen had invited the whole town to the ribbon-cutting ceremony. He tucked his speech in his pocket, grabbed his special scissors, and adjusted his tie. He wished he had on his official Ribbon-Cutting Tie.

The schoolyard was overflowing with people. Mr. Tanen made his way through the crowd.

Then he saw it!

Mr. Tanen's Playground

The playground was tied in a giant ribbon
made from Mr. Tanen's ties!

Mrs. Sweet Apple and Mr. Apple were at the microphone.

"Mr. Tanen, you have taught us all, 'The more you give, the more you get,'" said Mrs. Sweet Apple. "You have given us a playground. We are giving you back your ties."

With that, Mr. Apple untied
the tie ribbon and announced:
"Mr. Tanen's Playground is

NOW OPEN!"

33

Mr. Tanen and his ties
were together again!
He slipped on his Swing
and Slide Tie and smiled.

Saying Thank You

A Tie for Mr. Tanen

Imagine that you are one of the townspeople in *Mr. Tanen's Tie Trouble*. Work with a partner to make a tie to show Mr. Tanen how you feel about him. Will your tie have stripes, polka dots, or something else? Explain your design to your classmates. PARTNERS

Turn and Talk — Helping Out

Think about the problem that Mr. Tanen had. How did he get help from others to solve the problem? Look back at the story. Find two examples of how people helped Mr. Tanen. Tell a partner what you found. STORY STRUCTURE

Science

✔ **TARGET VOCABULARY**

received	chuckled
account	staring
budget	repeated
disappointed	fund

GENRE

Informational text gives facts about a topic. This is a science text.

TEXT FOCUS

Illustrations are pictures that show more about the text. As you read, look at the illustrations to help you understand the text.

Playground Fun!

Imagine staring out the window at a playground you designed yourself. That's exactly what kids in many communities have done. You can do it, too!

What would you include in your perfect playground? Would it have bridges, a slide, or talking tubes? Remember, if you design it yourself, you won't be disappointed!

Building a Playground

Kids in Highland Park, Michigan, helped design their playground. Then they received help from hundreds of people to get it built!

A playground starts with an idea. A budget shows how much money must be raised. People contribute money to the playground fund. The money is kept in a bank account. When there is enough money, volunteers build the playground.

Volunteers help build a playground in Michigan.

37

Totally Tubular!

Some playgrounds have talking tubes. If you chuckled into one end, a friend at the other end would hear you. If you repeated the laugh, they would hear you again.

How Talking Tubes Work

Sound travels as waves through the air. When people speak into a talking tube, their voice travels as sound waves through the air inside the tube.

Making Connections

 Text to Self

Write a Description Which of Mr. Tanen's ties do you like the best? Write a few sentences describing the tie you like and tell when a person might wear such a tie.

 Text to Text

Discuss Genre Think about *Mr. Tanen's Tie Trouble* and "Playground Fun!" Which tells facts? Which is a made-up story? Discuss your ideas with a small group.

 Text to World

Connect to Poetry Think about what you might see, hear, or feel at Mr. Tanen's playground. Write a poem about it. Use descriptive words.

Grammar

Pronouns A **pronoun** can take the place of a noun. To replace **nouns** that tell who or what is doing something, use the pronouns *I*, *he*, *she*, *it*, *we*, and *they*. To replace nouns that come after **verbs**, use the pronouns *me*, *him*, *her*, *it*, *us*, and *them*.

Nouns	Pronouns
The children want a new playground.	They want a new playground.
Mr. Tanen likes ties.	He likes ties.
My mother helped the principal.	My mother helped him.
The people bought all of the ties.	The people bought all of them.

Turn and Talk **Take turns with a partner. Name the pronouns that can replace the underlined nouns. Remember to speak only when it is your turn.**

1 Lou and Kim sat on the swings.

2 I like the slide.

3 My brother plays with sand.

Sentence Fluency When you write, try not to use the same subject over and over again. Use a pronoun to take its place. This will make your writing better.

Sentences with Repeated Subjects	Better Sentences
The two girls counted the money. The two girls hoped they had raised enough.	The two girls counted the money. They hoped they had raised enough.

Connect Grammar to Writing

When you revise your story paragraph, look for repeated words. Use pronouns to take their place.

Write to Express

Use details when you write a **story**. Details will help your reader picture what the story is about.

Ahmed drafted a story paragraph about a little boy who helped his mother. Later, he added some details to make his story more interesting.

Writing Traits Checklist

☑ Ideas

Did I add details to tell the reader more?

☑ Organization

Did I include a beginning, middle, and end?

☑ Word Choice

Do my words tell what the characters are feeling?

☑ Conventions

Did I use the way letters sound to help me spell words?

Revised Draft

Omar wanted to help his
mother. ʌHe came home early
one day fromʌthe park. His

She had been sick for a week.

playing with his friends in

mother was sitting at the
ʌtable. He wanted to do

kitchen

something to help.

Omar's Gift

by Ahmed Hakin

Omar wanted to help his mother. She had been sick for a week. He came home early one day from playing with his friends in the park. His mother was sitting at the kitchen table. He wanted to do something to help. He began to rinse the dishes and put them in the dishwasher. His mother looked at him and said, "You are a good son, Omar." She smiled at him. Omar knew that he had just given his mother a gift. It was a gift that made them both happy.

I added details to my final paper to make it more interesting.

Reading as a Writer

How do the details that Ahmed added tell his readers more? Where can you add details to your story?

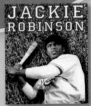

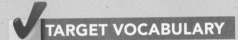
TARGET VOCABULARY

practice

hurried

position

roared

extra

curb

cheered

final

Vocabulary
Reader

Context
Cards

Vocabulary in Context

- **Read each Context Card.**

- **Make up a new sentence that uses a Vocabulary word.**

1 practice

If you practice hitting the baseball every day, your hitting will get better.

2 hurried

The soccer player hurried to stop the ball. He moved fast.

3 position

The batter is in position to hit the baseball.

4 roared

The crowd roared loudly as the player caught the ball.

5 extra

The extra players for the football team sat on the bench.

6 curb

After skating, the girl rested on the curb outside her house.

7 cheered

The audience clapped and cheered as the player scored a goal.

8 final

When the game ended, the final score was four to two.

Background

Early Baseball Many years ago, baseball was different from the way it is today. Teams could have extra players and innings. The runner had to be hit with the ball to be out!

Some things were the same as today. The teams had to practice, and each player had a position. Fans hurried across the curb to the field. The crowd cheered and roared for its team.

After the final game, a photographer took the team's photo.

46

Comprehension

✔ **TARGET SKILL** **Sequence of Events**

In *Luke Goes to Bat*, the author tells about Luke and the things that happen to him one summer. Putting these events in order in a chart like this can help you understand the story.

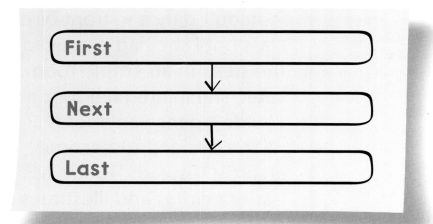

✔ **TARGET STRATEGY** **Visualize**

Use the information in your chart to help you form a picture in your mind of what happens in the story. You can also draw pictures of important events to help you.

Main Selection

Luke Goes to Bat

✓ TARGET VOCABULARY

practice	extra
hurried	curb
position	cheered
roared	final

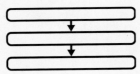
✓ TARGET SKILL

Sequence of Events
Tell the order in which things happen.

✓ TARGET STRATEGY

Visualize Picture what is happening as you read.

GENRE
Realistic fiction is a story that could happen in real life.

MEET THE AUTHOR AND ILLUSTRATOR
Rachel Isadora

Rachel Isadora grew up wanting to be a ballerina. She was so shy that she wouldn't dance in front of her class until she had practiced the steps in an empty room. Later, she injured her foot and couldn't dance anymore.

She decided to become an artist instead. Today, Ms. Isadora writes and illustrates children's books about ballet, music, and baseball.

LUKE GOES TO BAT

by Rachel Isadora

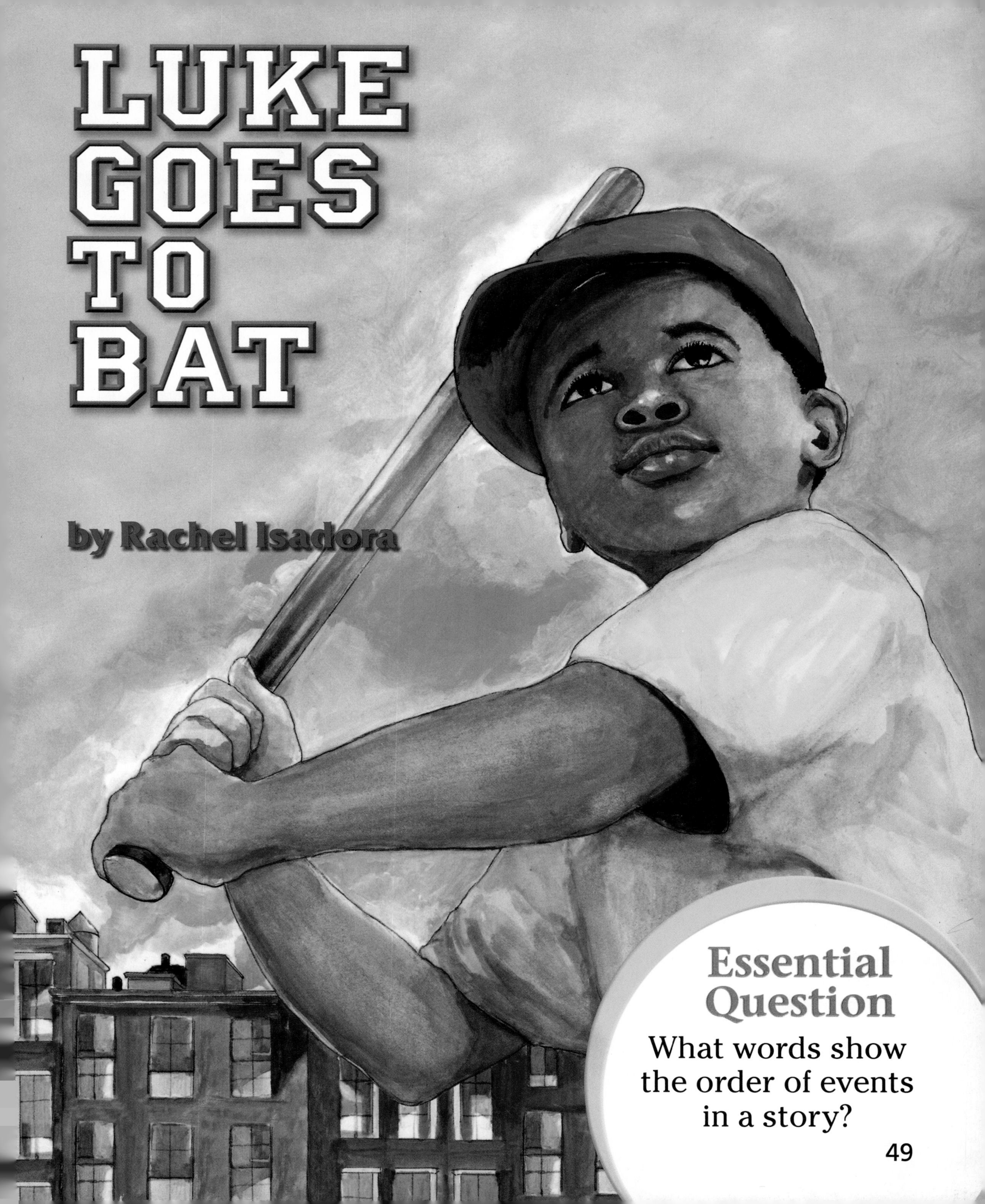

Essential Question

What words show the order of events in a story?

It was Brooklyn. It was summer.
It was baseball. All day long the kids on
Bedford Avenue played stickball in the
streets. Except for Luke.

"When you're older," his big brother, Nicky, told him.

"He's just a squirt," one of the other kids said, laughing.

So Luke watched the games from the curb, and then he'd practice.

He threw a ball against the wall next to the deli. He practiced his swing over and over again. He ran as fast as he could up and down the block.

He wanted to be ready when it was time.

And at night, whenever the Dodgers were playing, Luke hurried up to the roof, where he could see the lights of Ebbets Field. When he heard the crowd go wild, he imagined his favorite player, Jackie Robinson, had hit a home run.

Someday, Luke thought, I will hit a home run, too.

Finally, one morning, the team was short a player.

"Franky had to go to his aunt's!"

"Who we gonna get?"

"Hey," said Luke, "what about me?"

Everyone was quiet.

"Aw, come on," said his brother. "Give him a chance."

"We got nobody else."

"He better not mess up."

They put him in left field. No balls came his way, so he just stood there.

✓ STOP AND THINK
Sequence of Events
What happens that gets Luke into his first baseball game with the older boys?

When it was his turn up at bat, Luke took a
few practice swings, then stepped up to the plate.

"I'll show them," Luke muttered.

The ball whizzed past.

"Strike one!"

Luke held the bat higher.

"Strike two!"

Luke was barely in position when the next
ball flew past and the catcher yelled, "Out!"

55

"You stink," Luke heard.

He got up to bat one more time but struck out again.

"Sometimes it just goes that way," his brother told him.

Franky came back in the afternoon, so Luke spent the rest of the day on the curb. He was sure they'd never let him play again.

Grandma was in the kitchen when he got home.

"I finally got a chance to play with the team," Luke told her.

Grandma could tell that the game hadn't gone well. "Not everyone plays like Jackie Robinson all the time," she said. "Not even Jackie Robinson."

Luke didn't smile.

"By the way," Grandma said, "are you doing anything tomorrow night?"

Luke shrugged.

"Well, if you're so busy, someone else will have to go with me to the game at Ebbets Field."

"What? You mean a real game?"

Grandma held up two tickets.

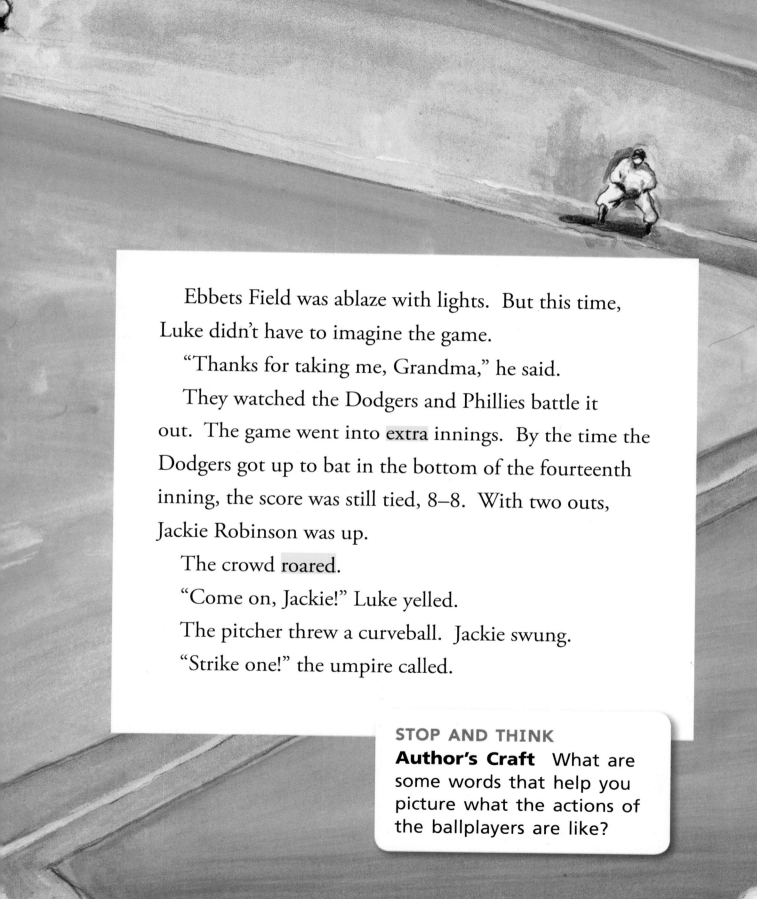

Ebbets Field was ablaze with lights. But this time, Luke didn't have to imagine the game.

"Thanks for taking me, Grandma," he said.

They watched the Dodgers and Phillies battle it out. The game went into extra innings. By the time the Dodgers got up to bat in the bottom of the fourteenth inning, the score was still tied, 8–8. With two outs, Jackie Robinson was up.

The crowd roared.

"Come on, Jackie!" Luke yelled.

The pitcher threw a curveball. Jackie swung.

"Strike one!" the umpire called.

STOP AND THINK

Author's Craft What are some words that help you picture what the actions of the ballplayers are like?

59

The pitcher wound up. He threw a fastball and Jackie missed.

"Strike two!"

Three balls followed.

All eyes at Ebbets Field rested on Jackie. The Dodgers could still win.

Luke shouted with the crowd. "Give it to 'em, Jackie! You show 'em!"

Jackie looked around from under his cap, then dug his feet into the dirt.

The pitcher began his windup. "You can do it, Jackie," Luke whispered. "You can do it."

Suddenly, Luke heard the loud crack of a bat. When he looked up, the ball was flying over his head, flying over the scoreboard, flying over the walls of Ebbets Field! The crowd went wild!

Luke stood up on his seat and cheered, "You showed 'em, Jackie!"

"What a game!" Grandma said. "See, you can't give up. Even Jackie Robinson's got to keep trying."

Luke didn't answer.

STOP AND THINK
Visualize How do the author and illustrator help you to see and hear the baseball park that night?

When Luke got home, he ran up to the roof. The lights were going out at Ebbets Field.

"Come on down! It's bedtime!" Nicky called.

Just then, Luke saw a ball lying on the ground.

"Look!" he said, picking it up. "This is the home run ball that Jackie Robinson hit tonight!"

"Naw. That's just some old ball a kid hit up on the roof," Nick said, laughing, as he went downstairs.

And that's when Luke saw him. It was Jackie Robinson himself.

"I hit that one for you, kid."

Before Luke could say a word, Jackie ran to the dugout to join the other Dodgers. But he looked back one more time.

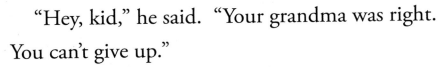

"Hey, kid," he said. "Your grandma was right. You can't give up."

"Thanks, Mr. Robinson."

The final lights went out at Ebbets Field. Luke looked down at the winning ball and smiled.

"I won't," he whispered to himself.

And he didn't.

Your Turn

Hooray for Heroes!

Hero Collage

Think about what it means to be a hero. Work with a small group to make a hero collage that shows people who are heroes or actions that are brave. You will need magazines, scissors, glue, and a large piece of paper. Share your finished collage with classmates. SMALL GROUP

Turn and Talk Beginning, Middle, or End?

Work with a partner. Choose several events from *Luke Goes to Bat* to act out. Take turns acting out the events for another set of partners to guess. Then tell if each event happened at the beginning, the middle, or the end of the story. SEQUENCE OF EVENTS

Technology

✔ **TARGET VOCABULARY**

practice	extra
hurried	curb
position	cheered
roared	final

GENRE

Informational text gives facts about a topic. This is a website.

TEXT FOCUS

A **website** is an online collection of pages about a topic. As you read, pay attention to how the website looks.

 **File** **Edit** **View** **Favorites**

JACKIE ROBINSON

Young Jackie

Jackie Roosevelt Robinson was born on January 3, 1919, in Cairo, Georgia. He and his family soon moved to Pasadena, California.

Jackie was good at sports, even as a young boy. He loved to run, play, and have fun with his friends.

Jackie was the youngest child in a family of athletes.

www.hmco.com   search

Jackie Grows Up

In high school and college, Jackie didn't sit on the curb and watch others play sports. He would practice a lot. Jackie was good at football, baseball, basketball, and track. Fans cheered for him when he played.

Into the Major League

In 1947, Jackie became the first African American to play Major League Baseball. Before that time, African Americans were not allowed to play in the major leagues.

Jackie played for the Brooklyn Dodgers. The position he played was second base. Fans would stay to watch him if a game went into extra innings. They roared when the team won.

Jackie was famous for stealing bases. In this photo, he hurried to get to home plate.

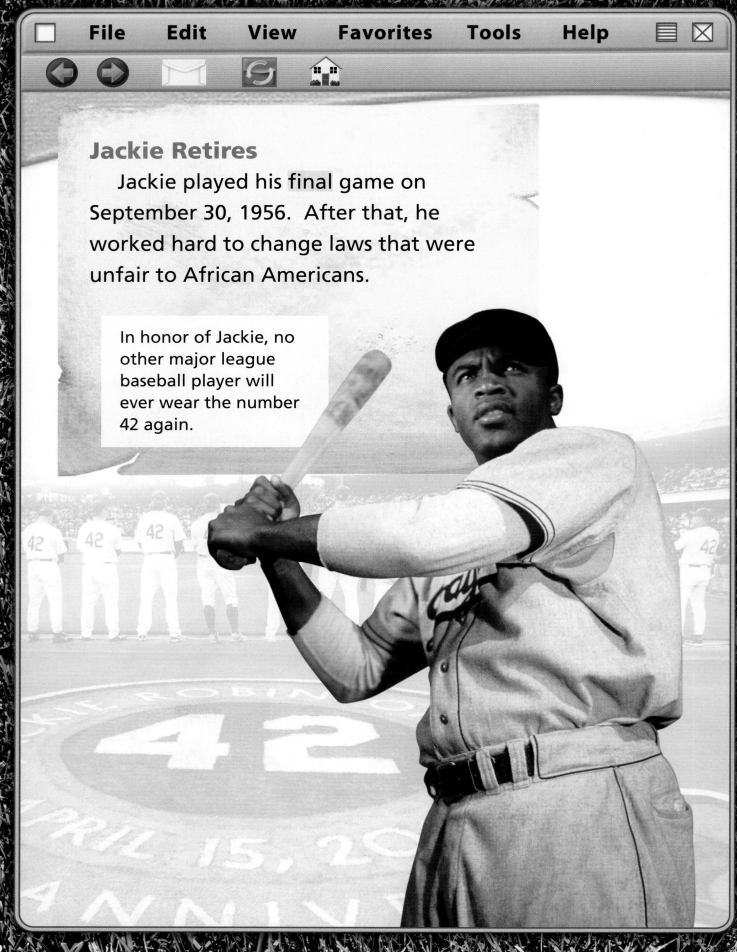

Jackie Retires

Jackie played his final game on September 30, 1956. After that, he worked hard to change laws that were unfair to African Americans.

In honor of Jackie, no other major league baseball player will ever wear the number 42 again.

Making Connections

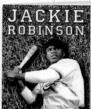

Text to Self

Write a Story Have you ever worked hard, as Luke did, to get good at something? Write sentences about your experience.

Text to Text

Discuss Purpose Think about why the authors wrote *Luke Goes to Bat* and "Jackie Robinson." How is the author's purpose for writing the story different from the author's purpose for making the website?

Text to World

Connect to Technology Luke watched baseball at Ebbets Field. How might seeing a game in person be different from seeing it on television? Share your opinion with a partner.

Grammar

Pronouns and Verbs A **verb** can name an action that is happening now. A **pronoun** can tell who or what is doing the action. If the pronoun *he*, *she*, or *it* comes before a verb that tells about now, add *-s* or *-es* to the verb. If the pronoun *we, I,* or *they* comes before a verb that tells about now, do not add *-s* or *-es*.

Academic Language

verb

pronoun

Add *-s* or *-es* to Verb	No Change to Verb
He hits the ball. She catches the ball. It breaks the window.	We hit the ball. I catch the ball. They break the window.

Try This! **Choose the correct verb to complete each sentence. Then write the sentence correctly.**

1. We (watch, watches) the game.

2. She (play, plays) well.

3. They (buy, buys) new bats.

4. It (roll, rolls) toward second base.

Conventions Edit your writing carefully. Make sure the verbs that go with the pronouns have the correct endings.

Singular Pronoun and Verb	**Plural Pronoun and Verb**
He looks at the ticket. She pitches to the batter.	We walk to the seats. They watch the game together.

✏️ Connect Grammar to Writing

When you edit your story paragraph, be sure you have written the correct verb to go with each pronoun.

Write to Express

Dialogue is what the characters say in a **story**. Dialogue can show what your characters are like.

Tandy drafted a story about a girl who meets a writer. Later, he added dialogue to show how his characters act and how they feel.

Writing Traits Checklist

✓ **Organization**
Do things happen in a way that makes sense?

✓ **Word Choice**
Did the words I chose show how the characters feel?

✓ **Voice**
Did I use dialogue to tell what the characters are like?

✓ **Sentence Fluency**
Did I use different types of sentences?

Revised Draft

"There he is!" Tonya shouted.
∧Tonya was going to meet her hero today. Shane Jonas was signing his books at the bookstore. Shane wrote stories about Tik and Tak. Tonya had read them all.
"Hi," Shane said as
∧Tonya and her dad walked up to
the table. ~~Shane Jonas~~ ∧"What's your name?" He reached out to shake her hand.

Tonya and Her Hero
by Tandy Haswell

"There he is!" Tonya shouted. Tonya was going to meet her hero today. Shane Jonas was signing his books at the bookstore. Shane wrote stories about Tik and Tak. Tonya had read them all.

"Hi," Shane said as Tonya and her dad walked up to the table. "What's your name?" He reached out to shake her hand.

"I'm Tonya, and this is my dad," Tonya said. "I love your books!"

"I love to hear that." Shane smiled and wrote a long note in her book.

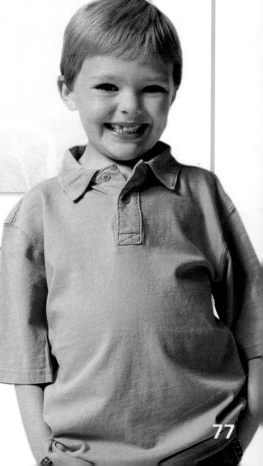

I added dialogue to tell more about what my characters are like.

Reading as a Writer

How does dialogue show more about the characters? Where can you add dialogue in your story?

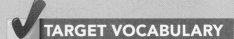
TARGET VOCABULARY

accepted

express

taught

grand

pretend

prize

wonder

fluttering

Vocabulary
Reader

Context
Cards

Vocabulary in Context

- Read each **Context Card**.

- Talk about a picture. Use a different Vocabulary word from the one in the card.

1 **accepted**

The student gave the teacher an apple. She accepted it.

2 **express**

You can express your ideas by writing a story.

3 taught

This teacher **taught** his class a new word.

4 grand

A **grand** award is a top prize in a contest.

5 pretend

This girl is not a real doctor. She is a **pretend** doctor.

6 prize

The best speller received first **prize** in the spelling bee.

7 wonder

The children **wonder** when the caterpillar will become a butterfly.

8 fluttering

The butterfly is **fluttering** its wings as it flies. The wings move quickly.

Background

✓ TARGET VOCABULARY **The Nobel Prize**

The Nobel Prize for Literature is a grand award. This important prize is given each year to a different writer. Gabriela Mistral received the prize in 1945. Some of her poems are about butterflies fluttering or pretend places. Mistral was also a teacher. She taught her students to express their feelings in words.

Do you wonder who will win the Nobel Prize for Literature next?

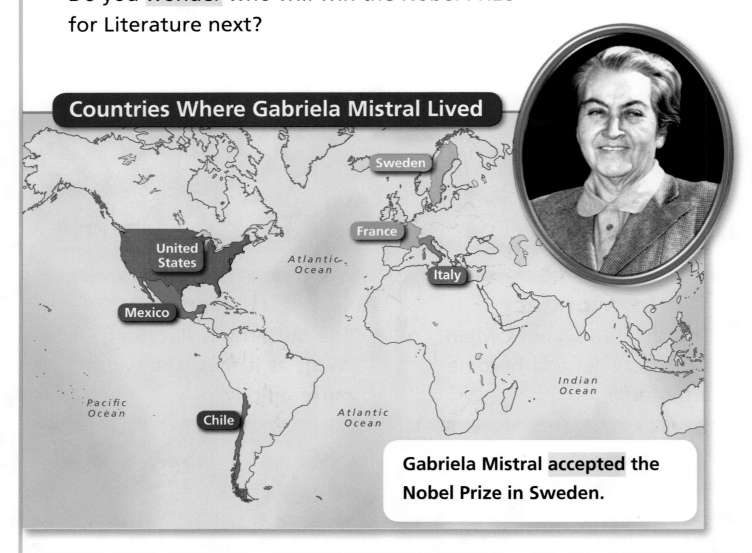

Countries Where Gabriela Mistral Lived

Sweden

France

United States

Italy

Mexico

Atlantic Ocean

Pacific Ocean

Chile

Atlantic Ocean

Indian Ocean

Gabriela Mistral accepted the Nobel Prize in Sweden.

Comprehension

✔ TARGET SKILL **Understanding Characters**

My Name is Gabriela is a true story about the poet
Gabriela Mistral. As you read the story, pay attention to
what Gabriela says and does. You can write important
details in a chart like this.

Words	Actions	Thoughts

✔ TARGET STRATEGY **Analyze/Evaluate**

Use the information in your chart and what you read
to decide why Gabriela became a teacher. This will
help you understand more about Gabriela Mistral.

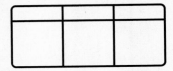

accepted	pretend
express	prize
taught	wonder
grand	fluttering

✔ **TARGET SKILL**

Understanding Characters Tell more about characters.

✔ **TARGET STRATEGY**

Analyze/Evaluate Tell how you feel about the text, and why.

GENRE

A **biography** tells about events in a person's life. Set a purpose for reading based on the genre.

MEET THE AUTHOR

Monica Brown

Monica Brown's daughters think it's pretty cool to have a mom who's an author. At book signings, "They'll walk up and announce that it was their Mommy who wrote this book," Ms. Brown says. The family lives in Arizona not far from the Grand Canyon.

MEET THE ILLUSTRATOR

John Parra

John Parra grew up in California in a home filled with Mexican art, food, and traditions. Today, Mr. Parra's colorful artwork can be seen in galleries, on posters and CD covers, and in the pages of children's books.

My Name is Gabriela

by Monica Brown   illustrated by John Parra

Essential Question

What makes a character interesting?

83

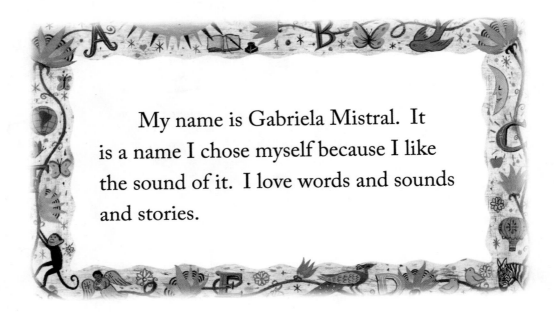

My name is Gabriela Mistral. It is a name I chose myself because I like the sound of it. I love words and sounds and stories.

GABRIELA MISTRAL

85

When I was a little girl, I lived with my mother and Emelina, my sister, in a small house in the beautiful Elqui Valley in Chile. From my bedroom window I could see the Andes Mountains.

When I couldn't sleep I would look up at the mountains and wonder what could be beyond them. Zebras with polka dots? Rainbow-colored flowers? Angels reading books?

I loved words—I liked the sounds they made rolling

off my tongue and I liked the

way they could express how I felt.

When I saw a butterfly fluttering, I noticed the way

the words fluttering butterfly sounded together—like a poem.

I taught myself to read so that I could read other people's words and stories. I read stories about princes and princesses, about monsters, and about birds and flowers.

STOP AND THINK
Author's Craft How does the author describe the way Gabriela feels about words?

89

I also liked to write poems, sing songs, and tell stories using the words that I knew. I told stories about happy times and sad times, about mothers and babies and little children.

I liked to play school with the children of my village.
I pretended to be the teacher, and my friends, Sofía, Ana,
and Pedro, were my pupils.

Pedro would always say that I was mean because I
made him write his ABCs until he knew all the letters
of the alphabet. But I told him that the alphabet is
important. How else would he create words and tell his
stories without it?

In our pretend class we sang songs like:
>The baby chicks are saying,
>Peep, peep, peep.
>It means they're cold and hungry.
>It means they need some sleep.

That was Sofía's favorite song. During recess we
had fun, running and chasing and laughing and playing.

When I grew up I became a real teacher and writer. I taught the children of Chile, and many of my students became teachers themselves.

I still wrote poems—happy poems, sad poems, stories of mothers and children. But I also wrote poems about animals—about parrots and peacocks and even rats!

 STOP AND THINK
Understanding Characters
What in the story tells you that Gabriela thinks teaching and learning are important?

I also traveled to far away places. I never saw
zebras with polka dots or rainbow-colored flowers,
but I met wonderful children and their teachers.
I traveled to Europe—to France and Italy.

I traveled to Mexico.

I traveled to the United States.

Everywhere I went, I wrote and taught and met teachers. I saw how all over the world, people wanted their children to learn.

My stories traveled the world with me. People liked
to read my happy stories, my sad stories, my stories of
women and children, my stories of parrots and peacocks,
of old lions and of the fisherfolk, who slept in the sand
and dreamt of the sea.

STOP AND THINK
Analyze/Evaluate What might Gabriela
Mistral want to tell children like you?

And because people from all over the world loved my stories so, I was given a very special prize—the Nobel Prize for Literature.

When I accepted the grand award, I thought of the beautiful mountains outside of my window in Chile, of my mother and sister, of the children of my village, and of all the stories that still need to be told.

Your Turn

What's in a Name?

Write a Name Poem

How would you describe Gabriela? Write a name poem. Use each letter in Gabriela's name to begin a word or set of words that describes her. Share your poem with the class.

PERSONAL RESPONSE

G reat writer
A lways following her dreams
B
R
I
E
L
A

Turn and Talk — Someone Special

Look back at pages 84–93 of the selection. Talk with a partner about Gabriela's actions as a child. Would you want to be her friend? Why or why not? UNDERSTANDING CHARACTERS

Poems About Reading and Writing

When you read a poem, do you pretend to be in the poem? When you write a poem, do you express wonder about things? These poems are about reading and writing.

Share the Adventure

Pages and pages
A seesaw of ideas—
Share the adventure

Fiction, nonfiction:
Door to our past and future
Swinging back and forth

WHAM! The book slams shut,
But we read it together
With our minds open

*by Patricia and
Fredrick McKissack*

The Period

Fat little period, round as a ball,
You'd think it would roll,
But it doesn't
At all.
Where it stops,
There it plops,
There it stubbornly stays,
At the end of a sentence
For days and days.

"Get out of my way!"
Cries the sentence. "Beware!"
But the period seems not to hear
    or to care.
Like a stone in the road,
It won't budge, it won't bend.
If it spoke, it would say to a sentence,
"The end."

by Richard Armour

Keep a Poem in Your Pocket

Keep a poem in your pocket
and a picture in your head
and you'll never feel lonely
at night when you're in bed.

The little poem will sing to you
the little picture bring to you
a dozen dreams to dance to you
at night when you're in bed.

So—
Keep a picture in your pocket
and a poem in your head
and you'll never feel lonely
at night when you're in bed.

by Beatrice Schenk de Regniers

Write a Poem

Write a poem about your favorite book.
Talk about how you might use rhythm, rhyme,
and repetition to make your poem fun to read.
Try to use the words accepted, grand, taught,
prize, and fluttering in your poem.

Making Connections

 Text to Self

Tell a Story How does Gabriela help people learn? How has a teacher made a difference in your life?

 Text to Text

Compare Heroes Remember what you learned about Helen Keller and Gabriela Mistral. How are these two women alike? Share your ideas with a partner. Remember to speak clearly.

 Text to World

Connect to Social Studies
Gabriela grew up in Chile. Use the index of a reference book to find an entry about Chile. Read the entry. Make two fact cards.

Chile is over 4,000 kilometers long from north to south.

Grammar

The Verb *be* The **verbs** *am*, *is*, and *are* tell about something that is happening now. The verbs *was* and *were* tell about something that happened in the **past**. Use *am*, *is*, or *was* if the sentence tells about one noun. Use *are* or *were* if the sentence tells about more than one.

Academic Language

verbs

past

Now	In the Past
I am tired.	I was awake last night.
Ann is a teacher.	Ann was a teacher last year, too.
The boys are in Chile.	The boys were in Mexico last week.

Try This! **Choose the correct verb to complete each sentence. Then write the sentence correctly.**

1. Gabriela (is, are) famous.

2. Her students (was, were) grateful.

3. Her books (is, are) easy to find.

4. My grandfather (was, were) a big fan.

Sentence Fluency You can combine sentences that have the same subject and verb. This will make your writing smoother.

Short, Choppy Sentences

The boy is a good reader.

The boy is a good writer.

Smoother Sentence

The boy is a good reader and writer.

Connect Grammar to Writing

When you revise your paragraph that describes, try combining sentences with the same subject and verb.

Write to Express

You can use sense words to tell how things look, feel, smell, sound, and taste.

Alice wrote a draft of a **description**. She wanted to tell about her favorite place. Later, she added sense words to make her description come alive.

Writing Traits Checklist

☑ **Ideas**
Did I show the reader what I mean?

☑ **Organization**
Did I start by telling what I am describing?

☑ **Word Choice**
Did I use sense words to tell more?

☑ **Conventions**
Have I combined ideas and sentences when I can?

Revised Draft

I love it at the beach. I
like walking on the soft, hot sand. I
love to listen to the pounding waves hit
the shore. The many smells
of spicy food make me hungry. My
brother usually buys me ~~an~~ a big, cool ice
cream cone. It always tastes delicious!

Our Summers at Long Beach

by Alice O'Brien

My family goes to Long Beach almost every summer. I love it at the beach. I like walking on the soft, hot sand. I love to listen to the pounding waves hit the shore. The many smells of spicy food make me hungry. My brother usually buys me a big, cool ice cream cone. It always tastes delicious!

> I used sense words to tell the reader more about how things look, feel, smell, taste, and sound.

Reading as a Writer

Which sense words did Alice add? What sense words can you add to your story?

✓ TARGET VOCABULARY

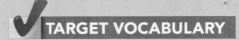

assistant

agreed

polite

failed

tearing

wisdom

cleared

trouble

Vocabulary Reader   Context Cards

Vocabulary in Context

● Read each **Context Card**.

● Ask a question that uses one of the Vocabulary words.

1 **assistant**

The assistant is helping to put up this sign.

2 **agreed**

The people agreed that this road needed a stop sign.

3 polite
This sign reminds children to be polite, or nice, to others.

4 failed
The sign failed to keep the dog off the grass.

5 tearing
The worker is tearing apart this old sign.

6 wisdom
The words of wisdom on this billboard teach us to act the right way.

7 cleared
The crossing guard cleared the way so these children could cross.

8 trouble
Without signs, drivers would have trouble knowing when to stop.

Background

✓ **TARGET VOCABULARY** **Why We Need Signs**

Without road signs, we would be in trouble. Road signs tell drivers to stop or go. If a driver failed to stop at a STOP sign, there could be an accident. Other signs say how fast a car can go. It is not safe or polite to drive over the speed limit. Tearing down road signs would be a bad idea. If you cleared away all signs, you would need an assistant to help put them up again!

People have agreed on the wisdom of obeying road signs such as these.

stop sign   traffic sign   safety sign

Comprehension

✓ **TARGET SKILL** **Text and Graphic Features**

In *The Signmaker's Assistant*, you must study the
pictures and read the signs to figure out what is
happening. A chart like this can help you keep track
of what the pictures tell you.

Text or Graphic Feature	Page Number	Purpose

✓ **TARGET STRATEGY** **Question**

Use the information in the chart to ask a question
about Norman and his signs. As you read, look for
the answer to your question.

assistant	tearing
agreed	wisdom
polite	cleared
failed	trouble

✓ **TARGET SKILL**

Text and Graphic Features Tell how words work with art.

✓ **TARGET STRATEGY**

Question Ask questions about what you are reading.

GENRE

Humorous fiction is a story that is written to make the reader laugh.

MEET THE AUTHOR AND ILLUSTRATOR

Tedd Arnold

When Tedd Arnold creates an illustration, he draws a scene with a pencil first. Next, using brown and blue watercolors, he paints shadows around the edges. He then paints lots of bright colors over the shadows.

The next step is rather unusual. Mr. Arnold makes tiny scribbles all over with colored pencils and outlines everything in black. It takes him two days to make each illustration.

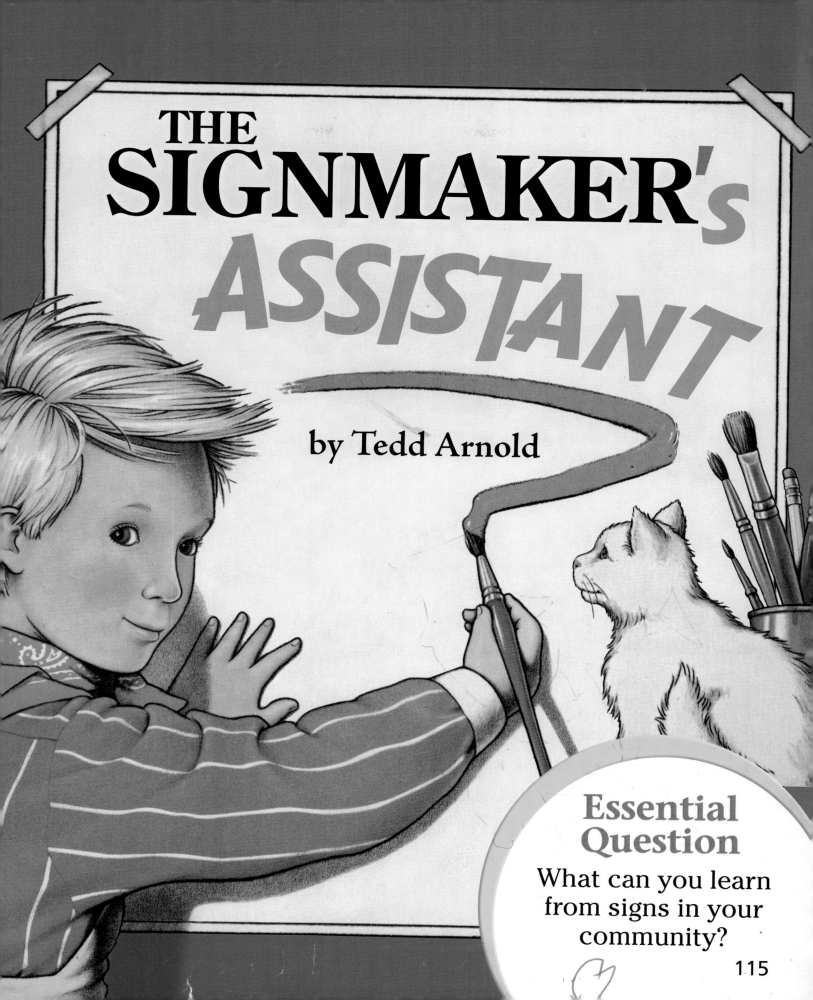

THE SIGNMAKER's ASSISTANT

by Tedd Arnold

Essential Question

What can you learn from signs in your community?

115

Everyone in town agreed. The old signmaker did the finest work for miles around. Under his brush ordinary letters became beautiful words—words of wisdom, words of warning, or words that simply said which door to use.

When he painted STOP, people stopped because the sign looked so important. When he painted PLEASE KEEP OFF THE GRASS, they kept off because the sign was polite and sensible. When he painted GOOD FOOD, they just naturally became hungry.

People thanked the signmaker and paid him well. But the kind old man never failed to say, "I couldn't have done it without Norman's help."

Norman was the signmaker's assistant. Each day after school he cut wood, mixed colors, and painted simple signs.

"Soon I will have a shop of my own," said Norman.

"Perhaps," answered the signmaker, "but not before you clean these brushes."

One day after his work was done, Norman stood at a window over the sign shop and watched people. They stopped at the STOP sign. They entered at the ENTER sign. They ate under the GOOD FOOD sign.

"They do whatever the signs say!" said Norman to himself. "I wonder . . ." He crept into the shop while the signmaker napped. With brush and board he painted a sign of his own.

Early the next morning he put up the sign, then ran
back to his window to watch.

"No school?" muttered the principal. "How could I
forget such a thing?"

"No one informed me," said the teacher.

"Hooray!" cheered the children, and everyone went home.

"This is great!" cried Norman. He looked around town for another idea. "Oh," he said at last, "there is something I have always wanted to do."

The following day Norman jumped from the top of the fountain in the park. As he swam, he thought to himself, I can do lots of things with signs. Ideas filled his head.

That afternoon when Norman went to work, the signmaker said, "I must drive to the next town and paint a large sign on a storefront. I'll return tomorrow evening, so please lock up the shop tonight."

As soon as the signmaker was gone, Norman started making signs. He painted for hours and hours and hours.

In the morning people discovered new signs all around town.

✔ STOP AND THINK
Text and Graphic Features
What makes Norman's signs so funny?

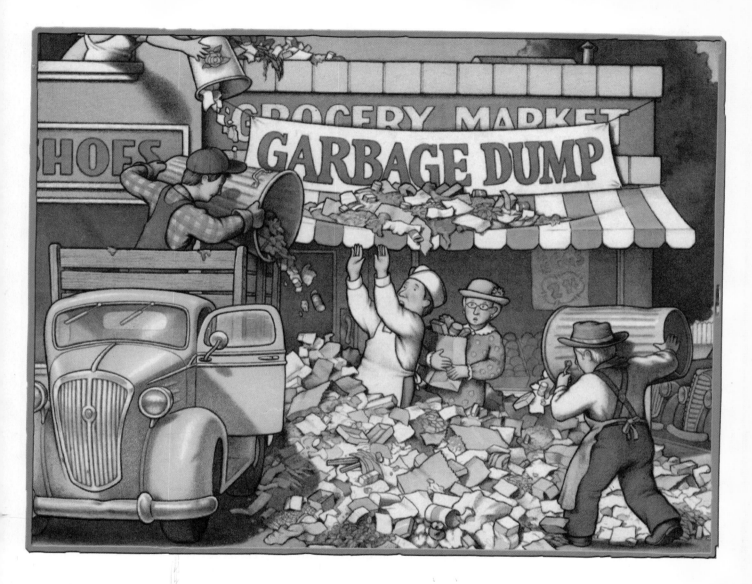

STOP AND THINK

Author's Craft Why does the author show rather than write about what the townspeople are doing?

Norman watched it all and laughed until tears came
to his eyes. But soon he saw people becoming angry.

"The signmaker is playing tricks," they shouted.
"He has made fools of us!"

The teacher tore down the NO SCHOOL
TODAY sign. Suddenly people were tearing down
all the signs—not just the new ones but every sign the
signmaker had ever painted.

Then the real trouble started. Without store signs, shoppers became confused. Without stop signs, drivers didn't know when to stop. Without street signs, firemen became lost.

STOP AND THINK
Question What question about the signs do these pages answer? What new questions do you have?

In the evening when the signmaker returned from his
work in the next town, he knew nothing of Norman's
tricks. An angry crowd of people met him at the back
door of his shop and chased him into the woods.

As Norman watched, he suddenly realized that
without signs and without the signmaker, the town was
in danger.

"It's all my fault!" cried Norman, but no one
was listening.

Late that night the signmaker returned and saw a
light on in his shop. Norman was feverishly painting.

DON'T BLAME THE SIGNMAKER.
I TRICKED YOU AND I'M SORRY.
— *Norman*

   While the town slept and the signmaker watched,
Norman put up stop signs, shop signs, street signs,
danger signs, and welcome signs; in and out signs, large
and small signs, new and beautiful signs. He returned all
his presents and cleared away the garbage at the grocery
store. It was morning when he finished putting up his
last sign for the entire town to see.

Then Norman packed his things and locked up
the shop. But as he turned to go, he discovered the
signmaker and all the townspeople gathered at the door.

"I know you're angry with me for what I did," said
Norman with downcast eyes, "so I'm leaving."

"Oh, we were angry all right!" answered the school
principal. "But we were also fools for obeying such signs
without thinking."

"You told us you are sorry," said the signmaker, "and you fixed your mistakes. So stay, and work hard. One day this shop may be yours."

"Perhaps," answered Norman, hugging the old man, "but not before I finish cleaning those brushes."

Your Turn

🎭 Act It Out

Write a Play

Think about how the signmaker and Norman treat each other. Work with a partner. Write a short play that shows how Norman and the signmaker act toward each other during one part of the story. Share your play with classmates.

PARTNERS

Turn and Talk — Sound Off About Signs

With a partner, look back through the story to find signs. Which signs were helpful to the people in the town? Which signs were not helpful? Which signs did you like best? Discuss your ideas together.   TEXT AND GRAPHIC FEATURES

✓ **TARGET VOCABULARY**

assistant	tearing
agreed	wisdom
polite	cleared
failed	trouble

GENRE

A **play** is a story people act out.

TEXT FOCUS

Stage directions in plays tell about the characters and setting. As you read, think about how the stage directions help you understand what the characters say and do.

The Trouble with Signs

by Bebe Jaffe

Cast of Characters
Ana

Ben

Ben: (steering a car) I'm glad we agreed to drive to the town meeting. We can look at the scenery.

Ana: (reading the pretend sign) Fresh berries. Turn left at the fork. Yum!

Ben: Where's the fork?

Ana: Do we need a fork to eat the berries?

Ben: I'm talking about a fork in the road!

Ana: I get it! You've got SO much wisdom, Ben.

Ben: I hope you are being polite and not teasing me.

Ana: (reading another sign) Do you have car trouble? Come to Polly's Place for some R and R. What's R and R?

Ben: R and R stands for Rest and Relaxation.

Ana: I'm glad that's cleared up, but do cars go to a special place for R and R?

Ben: (shaking his head) No, Ana. PEOPLE do.

Ana: Right! Listen to this sign! Have you failed in the kitchen? Are you tearing out your hair? Come to Carla's Cooking Class. Ouch! Do people tear their hair out because they overcooked a roast?

Ben: (losing patience) NO, Ana! That's just a saying. It means someone is getting frustrated.

Ana: Pull in! This is our meeting place.

Ben: Just in time! I'm tired of being your assistant.

Making Connections

 Text to Self

Make a Sign Which sign from *The Signmaker's Assistant* do you think is the silliest? Make a silly sign for your classroom using words and pictures. Display it for your class.

Make sure to laugh every 5 minutes!

 Text to Text

Talk About Signs Which signs would you rather see around your town, the signs Norman made or the signs from *The Trouble with Signs?* Explain.

 Text to World

Connect to Social Studies Look through *The Signmaker's Assistant* for signs that are helpful to people. Make a list with a partner, and talk about why the signs are important.

Grammar

Commas in Dates and Places Every day has a **date**. A date tells the month, the number of the day, and the year. Use a **comma** (,) between the number of the day and the year. Also use a comma between the name of a city or town and the name of a state.

Dates	Place Names
May 2, 2000	Austin, Texas
July 15, 2005	Westville, Idaho

Try This! **Write the underlined date or place correctly.**

❶ The signmaker opened his shop on <u>June 4 1975</u>.

❷ The shop was in <u>Tyler Texas</u>.

❸ The boy started work on <u>May 25 2007</u>.

❹ He came from <u>Logan Utah</u>.

Conventions Edit your writing carefully. Make sure you have used commas correctly when you write dates and names of places.

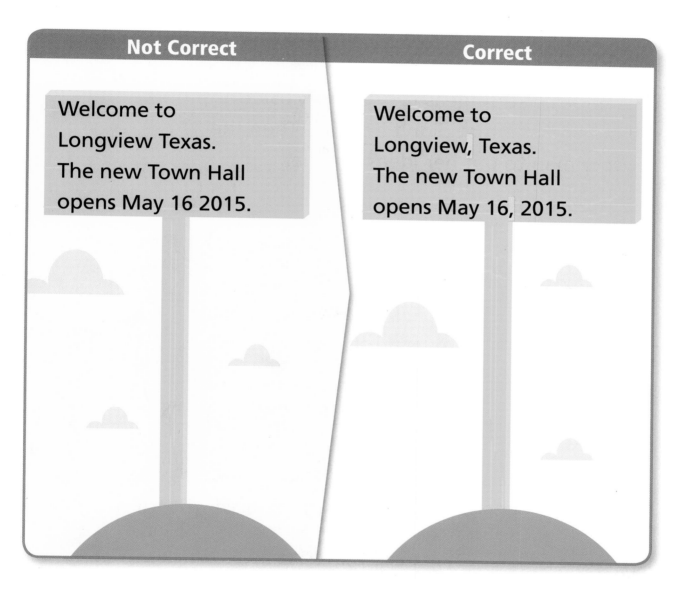

Not Correct	Correct
Welcome to Longview Texas. The new Town Hall opens May 16 2015.	Welcome to Longview, Texas. The new Town Hall opens May 16, 2015.

Connect Grammar to Writing

When you edit your story next week, be sure you have used commas, capital letters, and end marks correctly.

Write to Express

✔**Organization** A **story** has a beginning, middle, and end. The events in a story should be told in an order that makes sense.

Julie made a list of ideas for her story. She crossed out the one that didn't belong. Then she used a story map to put her ideas in order.

Writing Process Checklist

▶ **Prewrite**

✔ **Who are my characters?**

✔ **What happens at the beginning of the story?**

✔ **What happens in the middle?**

✔ **What happens at the end?**

Draft

Revise

Proofread

Publish and Share

Exploring a Topic

Girl has a pet.

~~She is a really good speller.~~

Pet has special powers.

They meet a sad giant.

Kids are afraid of the giant.

Hamster's name is Sparky.

Sparky knows when things are wrong.

Beginning

Layla and Sparky go to the park.
They see a sign that the park is closed.

Middle

They find a crying giant.
The giant tells them why he is crying.
Kids are scared of him.

End

The kids see how gentle the giant is
with Sparky.
The kids and the giant play together.

I put my ideas
in an order
that would
make sense
in my story.

Reading as a Writer

What differences do you see between
Julie's list and her story map? How
will putting your ideas in a story map
help you plan your story?

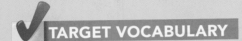

TARGET VOCABULARY

depended

sore

sprang

studied

gazing

hero

exercise

overlooked

Vocabulary Reader

Context Cards

Vocabulary in Context

- Read each **Context Card**.

- Tell a story about two pictures, using the Vocabulary words.

1 depended

The dog depended on its owner for food and water.

2 sore

The dog hurt its paw. The paw is sore.

3 sprang

The cat saw the food. She sprang toward her dish.

4 studied

Before getting a puppy, the girl studied a book about dog care.

5 gazing

This dog is gazing, or looking closely, at a squirrel.

6 hero

This dog is a hero. It saved the boy from getting hurt.

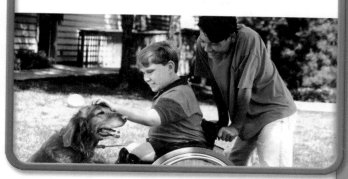

7 exercise

A dog needs exercise every day. This dog wants to run fast.

8 overlooked

They overlooked, or didn't see, where the dog was hiding.

Background

Hero Dogs Not every hero is human. Dogs may get overlooked, but people have often depended on them. People have studied dogs. They have given dogs exercise and training. Dogs can help people who have disabilities. Dogs can carry things for someone with a sore arm or leg. Some dogs have even saved people's lives!

The dog was gazing over as the boy stepped into the busy street.

The dog sprang up and nudged the boy aside.

What a hero!

Comprehension

In *Dex: The Heart of a Hero*, the author describes two animals named Dexter and Cleevis. Note ways the two are alike. Also find ways they are different. Use a Venn diagram like this to show your ideas.

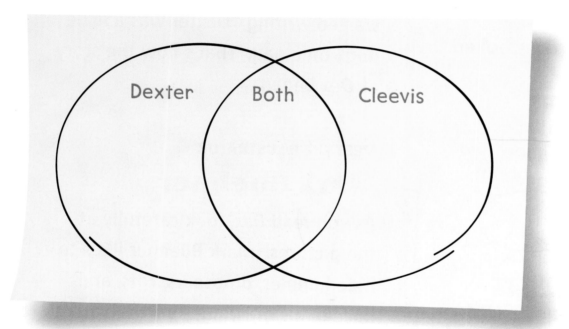

Dexter   Both   Cleevis

✔ **TARGET STRATEGY** **Monitor/Clarify**

As you read, monitor and clarify the ways Dexter and Cleevis are alike and different. Use what you know about each one to help make sense of the story.

depended	gazing
sore	hero
sprang	exercise
studied	overlooked

✓ TARGET SKILL

Compare and Contrast Tell how two things are alike or not.

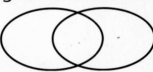

✓ TARGET STRATEGY

Monitor/Clarify Find ways to figure out what doesn't make sense.

GENRE

A **fantasy** is a story that could not happen in real life.

MEET THE AUTHOR

Caralyn Buehner

As the mother of nine children, Caralyn Buehner squeezes in time for writing whenever she can. Once, while waiting for her sons' karate class to end, she started writing "Dexter was a little dog" on a pad. That's how the story of *Dex* began.

MEET THE ILLUSTRATOR

Mark Buehner

As you read *Dex*, look carefully at the pictures. Mark Buehner likes to hide bunnies, dinosaurs, cats, and mice in his drawings. In case you're wondering, Mr. Buehner is Caralyn Buehner's husband, and their last name is pronounced *Bee-ner*.

DEX
The Heart of a Hero

by Caralyn Buehner
illustrated by Mark Buehner

Essential Question

How can stories be alike and different?

Dexter was a little dog. His legs were little, his tail was little, his body was little. He looked like a plump sausage sitting on four little meatballs.

Being the size that he was, Dex was often overlooked. The other dogs grew tired of waiting for Dex to catch up when they played chase, and after a while they forgot to invite him at all. No one really seemed to notice him, except when Cleevis, the tomcat, demonstrated how he could stand right over Dex and not even ruffle his fur.

Yes, everything about Dex was little—except for his dreams. He wanted to be a HERO. He could just *see* it.

THE MIGHTY DEX FLEW UP INTO THE DARK AND STARRY NIGHT. . . .

But *wanting* and *being* are two different things. Dex lived on dreams until one day, after crawling out from under Cleevis yet again, he decided there had to be more to life than gazing at the underside of a cat. There had to be more to *him*. If he *could* be a hero, he *would*!

So Dex started training. He read every superhero comic book he could find. He watched every hero movie ever made. He went to the library.

FURIOUSLY HE STUDIED, KNOWING EVERYTHING DEPENDED ON HIM. . . .

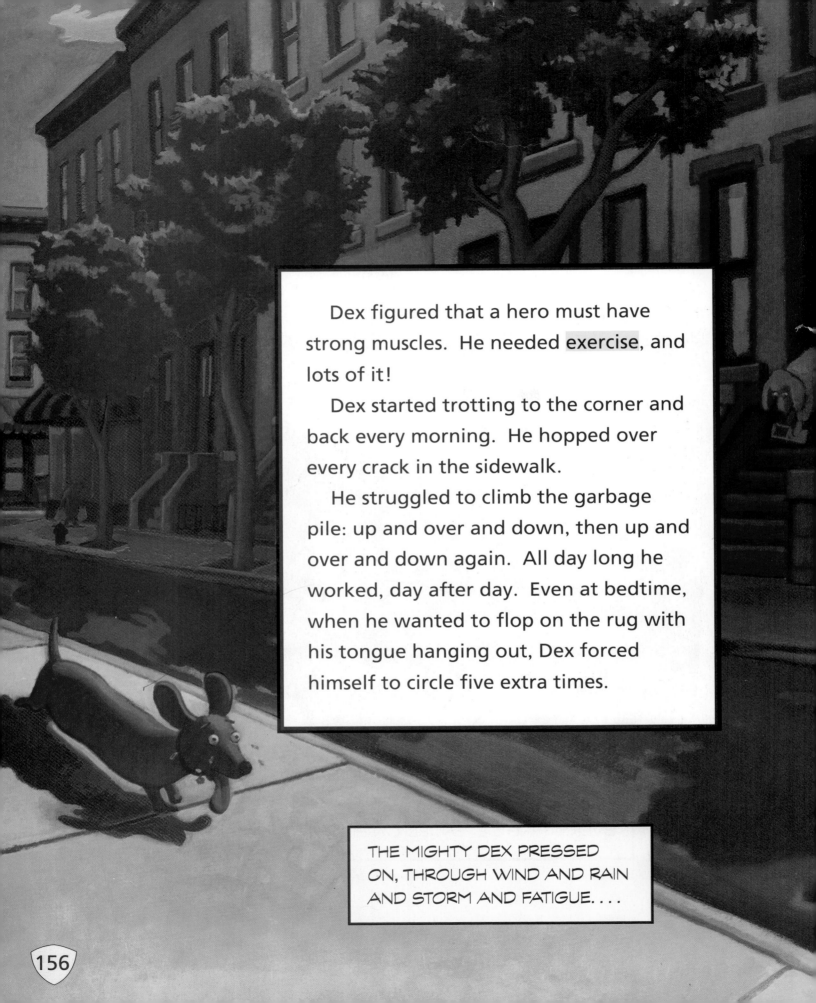

Dex figured that a hero must have strong muscles. He needed exercise, and lots of it!

Dex started trotting to the corner and back every morning. He hopped over every crack in the sidewalk.

He struggled to climb the garbage pile: up and over and down, then up and over and down again. All day long he worked, day after day. Even at bedtime, when he wanted to flop on the rug with his tongue hanging out, Dex forced himself to circle five extra times.

THE MIGHTY DEX PRESSED ON, THROUGH WIND AND RAIN AND STORM AND FATIGUE. . . .

156

When it got easier to run to the corner and back, Dex did it again, and then again. Then he dragged a sock filled with sand as he ran, and then *two* socks. When Cleevis was bored and stood in the middle of the sidewalk to block his way, Dex dropped to the ground and slid right under him. He was too busy to be bothered by Cleevis.

Dex was tired; he was sore. He was working so hard that he almost forgot what he was working for. But one night, as he dragged himself to bed after his last set of push-ups, Dex stopped in front of the mirror and flexed. He could feel them! He could see them! Muscles!

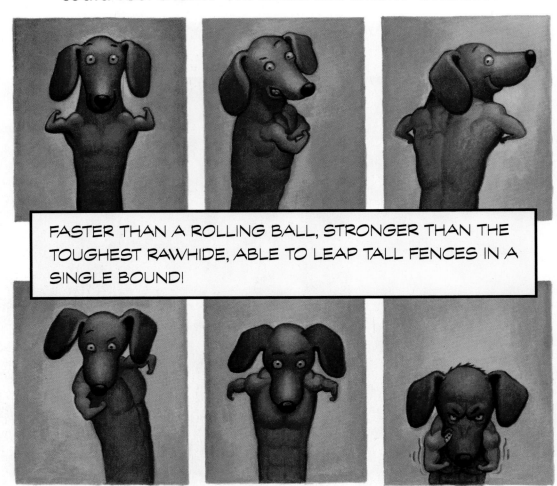

FASTER THAN A ROLLING BALL, STRONGER THAN THE TOUGHEST RAWHIDE, ABLE TO LEAP TALL FENCES IN A SINGLE BOUND!

Now Dex didn't "take" the stairs—he skimmed them! He leaped over hydrants; he vaulted up curbs. He could jump over the garbage mountain without touching the top! He could run like the wind; he felt as if his legs had springs!

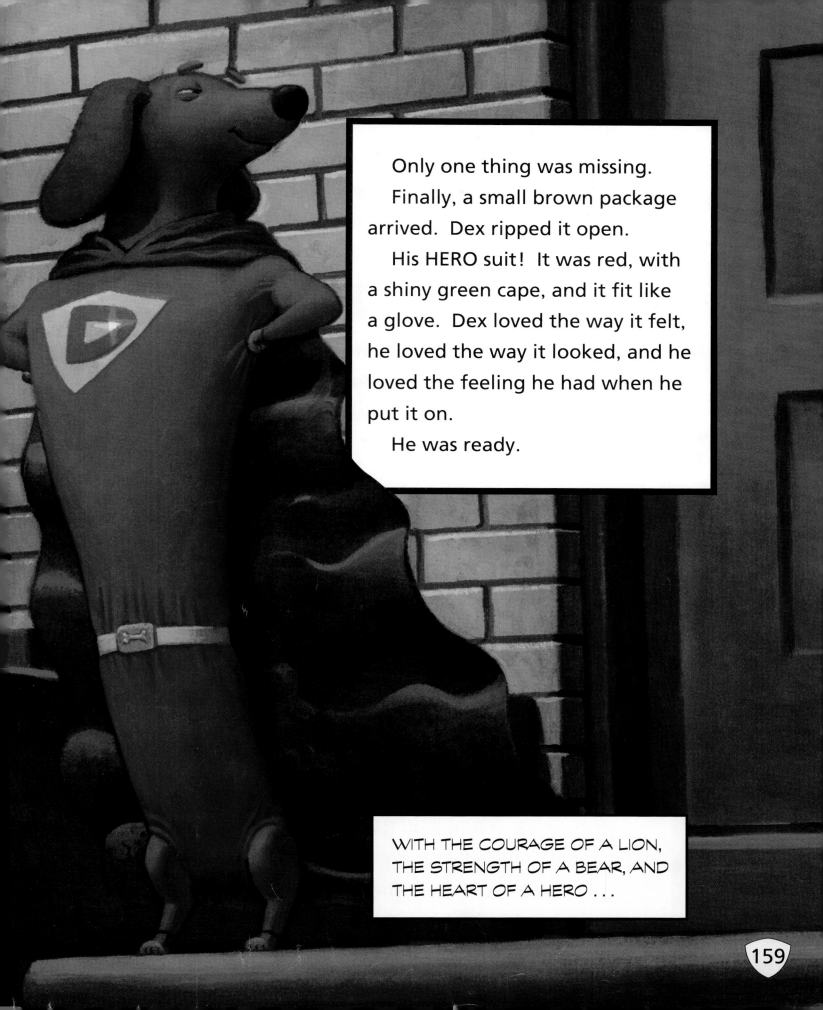

Only one thing was missing.

Finally, a small brown package arrived. Dex ripped it open.

His HERO suit! It was red, with a shiny green cape, and it fit like a glove. Dex loved the way it felt, he loved the way it looked, and he loved the feeling he had when he put it on.

He was ready.

WITH THE COURAGE OF A LION, THE STRENGTH OF A BEAR, AND THE HEART OF A HERO . . .

159

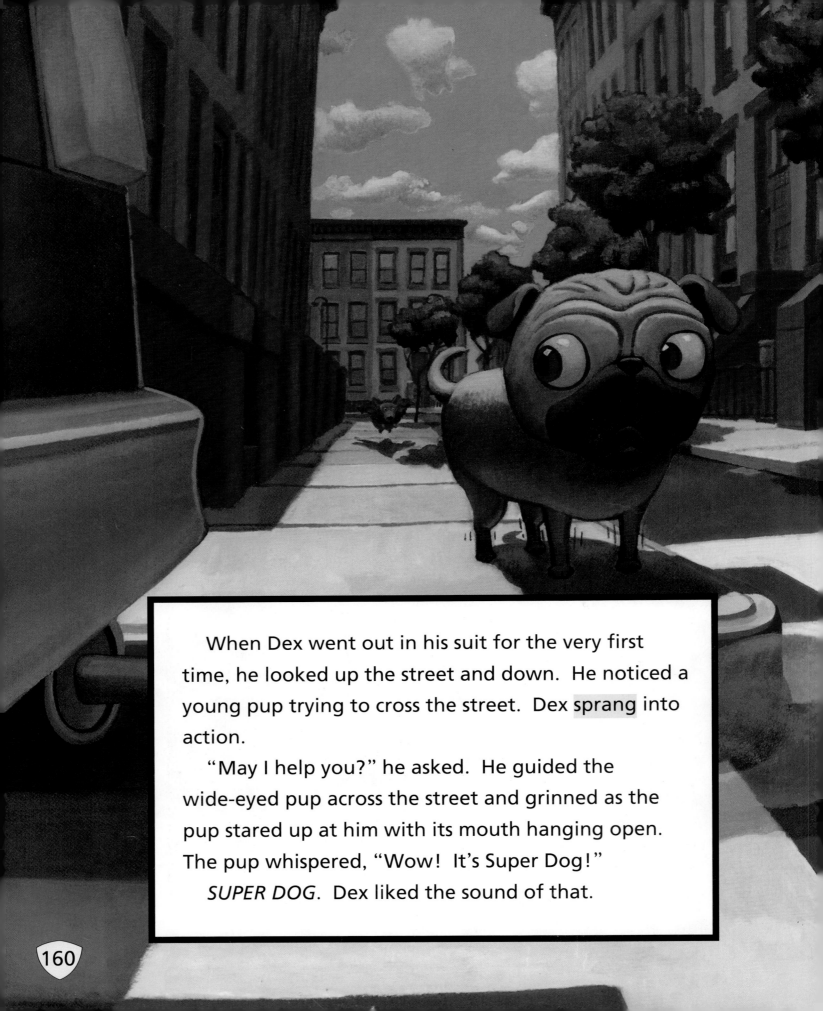

When Dex went out in his suit for the very first time, he looked up the street and down. He noticed a young pup trying to cross the street. Dex sprang into action.

"May I help you?" he asked. He guided the wide-eyed pup across the street and grinned as the pup stared up at him with its mouth hanging open. The pup whispered, "Wow! It's Super Dog!"

SUPER DOG. Dex liked the sound of that.

Of course, when Cleevis saw Dex, he just had to comment.

"Hey Dex, where's the party?"

Dex was so busy that he was able to ignore Cleevis— for the most part. The only time his face ever got red was when Cleevis yelled, "Where'd you get that dress-up?" Dex had to wonder if Cleevis saw anything but the suit. Didn't he understand that the suit was just a way to let people know he was there to help?

STOP AND THINK
Monitor/Clarify What do Dex's friends not understand about his suit?

There was a mouse he saved from a sewer,

a purse snatcher he tackled;

he fixed his neighbor's sprinkler;

he found a lost kitten, pulled a
rat away from a live wire,

tracked down a lost wallet,
put out a trash fire,

and organized a neighborhood
cleanup day.

It seemed that now, whenever anyone needed help,
they turned to Dex, and Dex had never been happier.

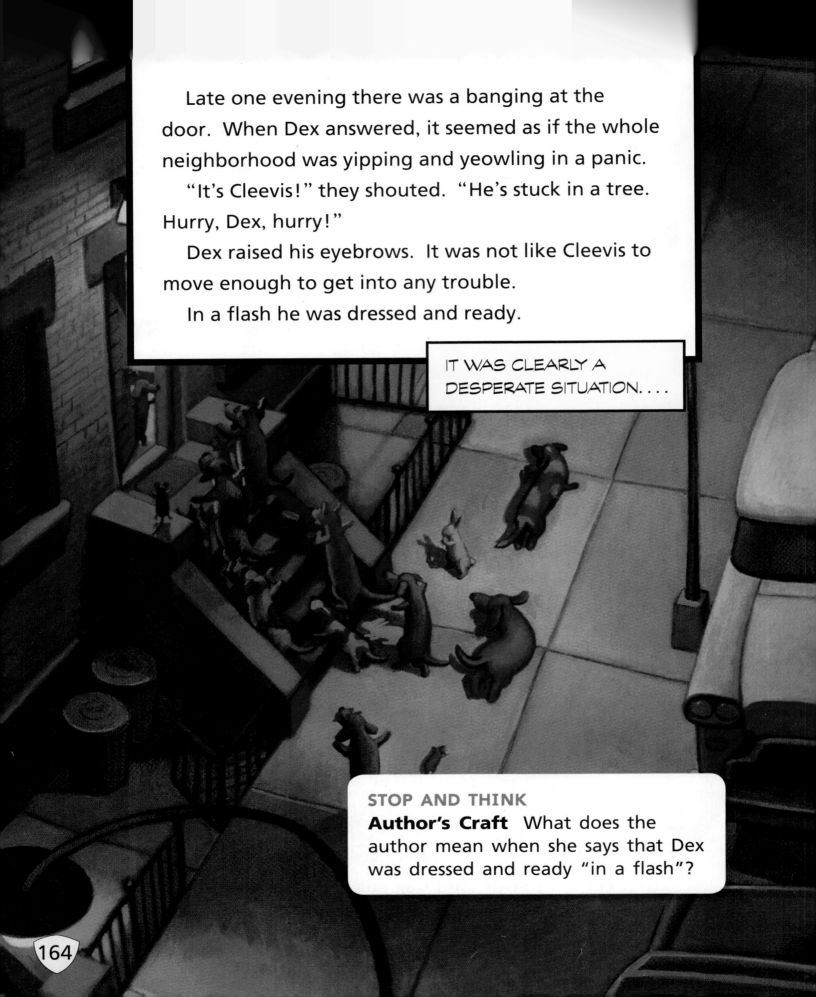

Late one evening there was a banging at the door. When Dex answered, it seemed as if the whole neighborhood was yipping and yeowling in a panic.

"It's Cleevis!" they shouted. "He's stuck in a tree. Hurry, Dex, hurry!"

Dex raised his eyebrows. It was not like Cleevis to move enough to get into any trouble.

In a flash he was dressed and ready.

IT WAS CLEARLY A DESPERATE SITUATION. . . .

STOP AND THINK

Author's Craft What does the author mean when she says that Dex was dressed and ready "in a flash"?

As he got closer, Dex could see Cleevis. He had been chasing a squirrel to the top of the tree, but had slipped and was hanging by one claw from a slender branch.

He was yeowling for all he was worth.

"I'm slipping!" Cleevis screeched. "Help me!"

Dex looked desperately around for something to climb on. There were no boxes or ladders, not even any trash cans. Then Dex looked at the crowd.

"Quick, everybody!" Dex shouted. "I've got an idea!" Dex leaped onto the end of the teeter-totter facing the tree, pushing it to the ground.

"Everybody on the other end! One! Two! Three!!!!"

All the animals jumped together on the other end of the teeter-totter, catapulting Dex into the air. He soared over the crowd, his ears and cape streaming out behind him. . . .

THE MIGHTY DEX FLEW UP INTO
THE DARK AND STARRY NIGHT. . . .

Dex scrambled onto the branch next to
Cleevis. Quickly he pulled off his cape and tied
its four corners onto the screeching cat.
  "Jump!" Dex shouted. "Jump, Cleevis!"

With an ear-piercing shriek, Cleevis let go. The billowing cape caught the air and parachuted the big cat to the ground. Dex backed up and slid to the ground amidst the cheers of the crowd.

Dex was bruised and tired, but he forgot his discomfort as Cleevis sheepishly lumbered over, still tangled in the green cape.

"Thanks, Dex. You really are a hero!"

Dex didn't think he could feel any better, but he did—just a little—the next day, when Cleevis sidled up next to him and whispered, "Say, Dex, could I be your partner?"

Dex looked the big tomcat up and down. It would take a *lot* of work to turn Cleevis into a hero. He could hardly wait.

"Sure," said Dex with a grin. "Sure."

WITH TWICE THE BRAINS AND TRIPLE THE BRAWN, OUR HEROES FORGE ON, EVER READY TO LEND A HELPING PAW!

✓ **STOP AND THINK**
Compare and Contrast How has Cleevis changed by the end of the story?

Your Turn

Story Review

Write an E-Mail

Think about the parts you liked best in *Dex: The Heart of a Hero*. Did you like the illustrations, the characters, or the story itself? Write an e-mail to a friend. Explain which parts of the story you liked and why. AUTHOR'S CRAFT

Turn and Talk — Superhero Stories

Think of other superhero stories that you know. How is Dex like the superheroes in those stories? How is he different? Talk about this with a partner. Give examples. COMPARE AND CONTRAST

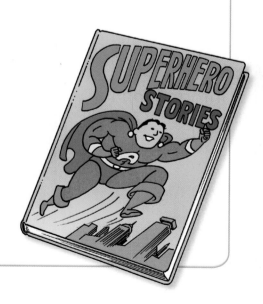

✓ TARGET VOCABULARY

depended	gazing
sore	hero
sprang	exercise
studied	overlooked

GENRE
Informational text gives facts about a topic. This is a social studies text.

TEXT FOCUS
A **chart** is a drawing that lists information in a clear way.

HEROES THEN AND NOW

What makes a hero? A hero does something brave or works hard to help others. A hero doesn't give up when things are hard.

Heroes are important people, whether they lived in the past or do good deeds today.

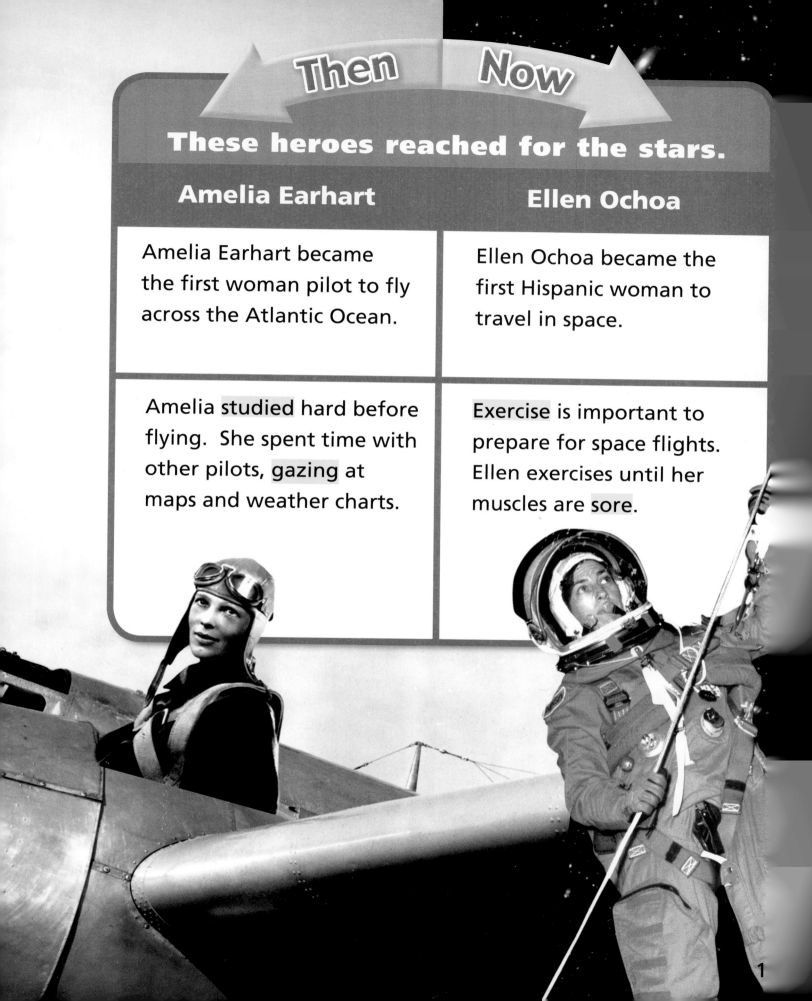

Then / Now

These heroes reached for the stars.

Amelia Earhart	Ellen Ochoa
Amelia Earhart became the first woman pilot to fly across the Atlantic Ocean.	Ellen Ochoa became the first Hispanic woman to travel in space.
Amelia studied hard before flying. She spent time with other pilots, gazing at maps and weather charts.	Exercise is important to prepare for space flights. Ellen exercises until her muscles are sore.

Then / Now

The heroes in this chart helped others.

Olga Kohlberg	Muhammad Yunus
More than 100 years ago, Olga Kohlberg **sprang** into action to help people learn. She started a kindergarten in Texas. She also helped start public libraries.	Muhammad Yunus is working hard to end poverty in Bangladesh. He built a bank. Now people can borrow money to build houses and start businesses.
Many children and adults **depended** on Olga. 	Muhammad has not **overlooked** the poor. He helps them succeed. 

Making Connections

Text to Self

Share a Story Think of a time when you felt the way Dex does at the beginning of *Dex: The Heart of a Hero*. What did you do? Tell a partner.

Text to Text

Connect to Poetry Think about Dex and the heroes you read about in "Heroes Then and Now." What makes them heroes? Use some of your senses to write a short poem about a hero.

Text to World

Dog Heroes What does Dex do to help the other animals? What are some ways dogs can help in your community? Talk about this with your class.

Grammar

Commas in a Series When there are three or more **nouns** in a sentence, separate them with **commas** and the word *and*. Also use commas and the word *and* when there are three or more **verbs** in a sentence.

Academic Language

nouns

commas

verbs

Series of Nouns	Series of Verbs
The dogs, cats, and birds saw Dex.	He jumped, hopped, and ran to help.
My sister, my brother, and I want to be heroes.	We stretch, flex, and train our muscles.

Turn and Talk **Read the sentences aloud with a partner. Tell where to add commas to make the sentences correct. Use complete sentences as you talk to your partner.**

1 The cat scratched howled and hissed.

2 Dex helped boys girls and animals.

3 He studied ran and practiced.

Sentence Fluency Short, choppy sentences can be combined. This will make your writing smoother.

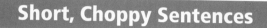
Short, Choppy Sentences

The dog leaped over boxes.

The dog leaped over logs.

The dog leaped over fences.

Smoother Sentence with Commas

The dog leaped over boxes, logs, and fences.

Connect Grammar to Writing

When you revise your story, try combining some short sentences.

Write to Express

✓**Organization** A good **story** starts with a strong beginning. If the beginning of your story is interesting, it makes your readers want to read more.

Julie wrote a draft of a story about a girl and her special pet. Later, she revised the story's beginning.

Writing Process Checklist

Prewrite

Draft

▶ **Revise**

✓ Does my story have a beginning, middle, and end?

✓ Does the beginning make the reader want to read more?

✓ Did I include interesting details?

✓ Did I tell how the problem is solved?

Edit

Publish and Share

Revised Draft

Layla had a pet hamster named

Sparky. Sparky was not like any
other hamster. He could do something no other
∧ hamster could do.

Sparky was small and brown.
He had a little black nose.
He was amazing because he knew
∧

when things were wrong.

Sparky and the Giant

by Julie Martine

Layla had a pet hamster named Sparky. Sparky was not like any other hamster. He could do something no other hamster could do.

Sparky was small and brown. He had a little black nose. He was amazing because he knew when things were wrong.

One day Layla and Sparky were walking in the park. Sparky started making noise and running around in Layla's pocket.

"What's up, Sparky?" Layla said as she patted her pocket.

I made the beginning more interesting.

Reading as a Writer

How does Julie make her beginning more interesting? How can your beginning be more interesting?

Read the next two selections. Think about the order of events in each selection.

The Cattle Queen

Lizzie Johnson moved to Texas as a young girl. Her parents started a school. She later became a teacher in that school. Then she started her own school in Austin.

About this time, many cattle owners were taking their herds north. They drove them up the Chisholm Trail. This trail went up to the railroad in Kansas. Cattle were sold there. Lizzie was a sharp woman. She saw men making a lot of money. She decided to start her own cattle business.

Lizzie became the first woman in Texas to ride the Chisholm Trail with a herd of her own longhorn cattle.

A Cowboy's Life

During the late 1800s, many Texan cowboys took part in long cattle drives. They moved herds of cattle from one place to another. It sometimes took three months.

Cowboys had to work to keep the herd together during the cattle drive. On sunny days, it was hot and dusty. On rainy days, it was cold and wet.

Cowboys faced many dangers. They had to cross deep water. They had to watch out for hazards, such as lightning and rattlesnakes.

Cowboys rode from sunrise to sunset. At night, they gathered around a fire. They told stories and sang. Each cowboy took a two-hour shift to watch the cattle.

Unit 4 Wrap-Up

The Big Idea

Make a Difference
How can you help another person? Write instructions showing how to help someone do something, such as set a table or ice-skate.

1. Stretch your arms out for balance.
2. Push with one foot.
3. Glide with the other foot.
4. You're skating!

Listening and Speaking

My Favorite Hero Think about all the heroes in this unit. Was Jackie Robinson your favorite? Did you think Mr. Tanen, Gabriela, or Norman were heroes? Did you like Dexter the Super Dog the best? Talk with a partner about which one was your favorite hero and tell why.

Changes, Changes Everywhere

unit 5

Big Idea

Living things change over time.

Paired Selections

Lesson

21

Penguin Chick
**Narrative Nonfiction:
Science**
page 190

Animal Poems
Poetry
page 208

Lesson

22

Gloria Who Might Be My Best Friend
Realistic Fiction
page 220

How to Make a Kite
**Informational Text:
Science**
page 238

Lesson

23

The Goat in the Rug
Narrative Nonfiction
page 250

Basket Weaving
**Informational Text:
Social Studies**
page 270

Lesson

24

Half-Chicken
**Folktale:
Traditional Tales**
page 282

The Lion and the Mouse
**Folktale:
Traditional Tales**
page 300

Lesson

25

How Groundhog's Garden Grew
Fantasy
page 312

Super Soil
**Informational Text:
Science**
page 334

Lesson 21

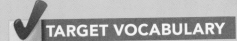

TARGET VOCABULARY

webbed

waterproof

steer

whistle

otherwise

junior

slippery

finally

Vocabulary Reader   Context Cards

186

Vocabulary in Context

- Read each **Context Card**.
- Place the Vocabulary words in alphabetical order.

1 webbed

A penguin is a bird with big, webbed feet. Its toes are joined by thin skin.

2 waterproof

Penguins' feathers are waterproof, which keeps the birds warm and dry.

3 steer

Webbed feet help penguins **steer** through the cold Antarctic water.

4 whistle

It is very cold in Antarctica. The wind makes a high, sharp sound, like a **whistle**.

5 otherwise

The penguin father keeps his egg warm. **Otherwise**, the egg might get too cold.

6 junior

At five months, a **junior** penguin is still younger than an adult.

7 slippery

The scientist tries not to slide on the ice. The ice is very **slippery** to walk on.

8 finally

These penguin chicks **finally** grew up and became adult penguins.

Background

Antarctica Antarctica is a
cold, windy place. It is covered with slippery ice and
snow. Seals have extra fat to keep warm. Birds have
waterproof feathers. Otherwise, they could freeze.
Most animals get their food from the sea. To help them
steer as they swim, emperor penguins have webbed
feet. Junior penguins call to parents with a whistle.
Once grown, the young penguins are finally ready to
live on their own.

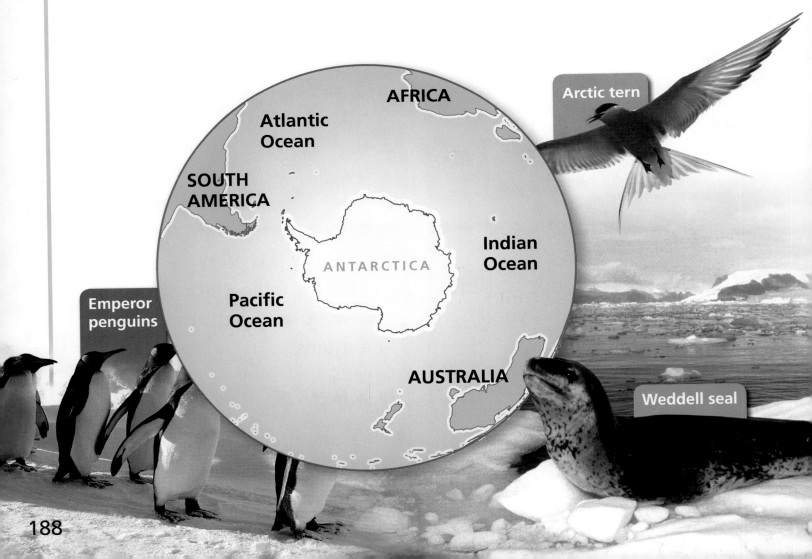

AFRICA

Atlantic
Ocean

SOUTH
AMERICA

Indian
Ocean

ANTARCTICA

Arctic tern

Emperor
penguins

Pacific
Ocean

AUSTRALIA

Weddell seal

Comprehension

✔ **TARGET SKILL** **Main Ideas and Details**

A topic is what a selection is about. The most important ideas are called main ideas. Details tell more information about main ideas. Use the title page to help you figure out the topic of *Penguin Chick*. As you read, use a chart to show a main idea and the details about it.

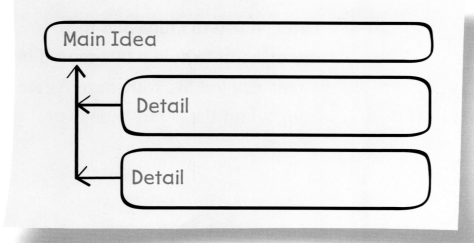

✔ **TARGET STRATEGY** **Infer/Predict**

Use the details and main ideas in *Penguin Chick* to help you figure out more about penguin chicks. Also use details to infer what it is like to live in Antarctica.

JOURNEYS DIGITAL | Powered by DESTINATIONReading
Comprehension Activities: Lesson 21

Main Selection

TARGET VOCABULARY

webbed	otherwise
waterproof	junior
steer	slippery
whistle	finally

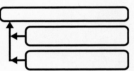
TARGET SKILL
Main Ideas and Details Tell important ideas and details about a topic.

TARGET STRATEGY
Infer/Predict Use clues to figure out more about story parts.

GENRE
Narrative nonfiction tells a true story about a topic. Set a purpose for reading based on the genre.

MEET THE AUTHOR
Betty Tatham
"I only write about subjects I love, or those I want to learn more about," says Betty Tatham. Penguins are her favorite animal, so she wrote *Penguin Chick*. After seeing playful otters at the Monterey Bay Aquarium in California, she wrote *Baby Sea Otter*. A trip to China and the opportunity to hold a five-month-old panda cub led Ms. Tatham to create a book about these rare animals.

Penguin Chick

by Betty Tatham

Essential Question

How do you know which facts are important?

191

A fierce wind howls. It whips snow across the ice.
Here, a female emperor penguin has just laid an egg.
It is the only egg she will lay this year.

Most birds build nests for their eggs. But on the ice in
Antarctica, there are no twigs or leaves. There is no grass
or mud. Nothing to build a nest with. Nothing but snow
and ice.

The new penguin father uses his beak to scoop the egg onto his webbed feet.

He tucks it under his feather-covered skin, into a special place called a brood patch. The egg will be as snug and warm there as if it were in a sleeping bag.

One of the penguin parents must stay with the egg to keep it warm. But where penguins lay their eggs, there is no food for them to eat.

The penguin father is bigger and fatter than the mother. He can live longer without food. So the father penguin stays with the egg while the mother travels to the sea to find food.

The two parents sing together before the mother penguin leaves.

Along with many other penguins, the mother penguin leaves the rookery, where she laid her egg.

The mother walks or slides on her belly. This is called tobogganing. She uses her flippers and webbed feet to push herself forward over ice and snow.

Because it's winter in Antarctica, water near the shore is frozen for many miles. After three days the mother penguin comes to the end of the ice. She dives into the water to hunt for fish, squid, and tiny shrimplike creatures called krill.

Back at the rookery, the penguin fathers form a group called a huddle. They stand close together for warmth. Each one keeps his own egg warm.

For two months the penguin father always keeps his egg on his feet. When he walks, he shuffles his feet so the egg doesn't roll away. He sleeps standing up. He has no food to eat, but the fat on his body keeps him alive.

> ✔ **STOP AND THINK**
> **Main Ideas and Details** What is the main idea on this page? Which details support the main idea?

Finally he feels the chick move inside the egg. The chick pecks and pecks and pecks. In about three days the egg cracks open.

The chick is wet. But soon his soft feathers, called down, dry and become fluffy and gray. The father still keeps the chick warm in the brood patch. Sometimes the chick pokes his head out. But while he's so little, he must stay covered. And he must stay on his father's feet. Otherwise the cold would kill him.

The father talks to the chick in his trumpet voice. The chick answers with a whistle.

STOP AND THINK
Author's Craft Why does the author use the words **trumpet** and **whistle**?

The father's trumpet call echoes across the ice. The penguin mother is on her way back to the rookery, but she can't hear him. She's still too far away. If the mother doesn't come back soon with food, the chick will die.

Two days pass before the mother can hear the father penguin's call.

At last the mother arrives at the rookery. She cuddles close to her chick and trumpets to him. He whistles back. With her beak she brushes his soft gray down.

The mother swallowed many fish before she left the ocean. She brings some of this food back up from her stomach and feeds her chick. She has enough food to keep him fed for weeks. He stays on her feet and snuggles into her brood patch.

The father is very hungry, so he travels to open water. There he dives to hunt for food. Weeks later the father returns with more food for the chick.

Each day the parents preen, or brush, the chick's downy coat with their beaks. This keeps the down fluffy and keeps the chick warm.

STOP AND THINK
Infer/Predict What has the father done so far? What do you think he will do next?

As the chick gets bigger, he and the other chicks no longer need to stay on their parents' feet. Instead they stay together to keep warm.

This group of chicks is called a crèche, or a nursery. The chick now spends most of his time here. But he still rushes to his mother or father to be fed when either one comes back from the ocean.

Sometimes the chick and the other young penguins dig their beaks into the ice to help them walk up a slippery hill. They toboggan down fast on their fluffy bellies.

The chick grows and grows. After five months, he has grown into a junior penguin. He is old enough to travel to the ocean.

Now he has a waterproof coat of feathers, instead of fluffy down. He can swim in the icy cold ocean because his feathers keep him dry and warm.

The young penguin spends most of his time in the water. He swims, flapping his flippers as if he were flying underwater. He uses his webbed feet to steer wherever he wants to go.

He catches a fish with his beak and swallows it headfirst.

Now the young penguin can catch his own food and take care of himself. In about five years he'll find a mate. Then he'll take care of his own egg until the chick can hatch.

Your Turn

🔍 Land for Sale

Write an Ad

Imagine that you are selling land to penguins in Antarctica. With a small group, write an ad for the land you want to sell. Be sure to include in your ad all the things a penguin chick needs to survive.

SMALL GROUP

Turn and Talk — Fact Hunt

Look back through *Penguin Chick.* Choose two facts that you find interesting. Share your facts with a partner. Explain how each fact helps support the selection's main idea.

MAIN IDEA AND DETAILS

Readers' Theater

Animal Poems

Reader 1: Here's a poem about animals that have webbed feet and waterproof feathers! They are birds, but they don't have a song or a whistle.

Reader 2: Let's read this poem together.

Quack?

Quack sound is crisp,
Crackly-quick
As the snap of teeth
On a celery stick.
Do you think ducks
Ever feel absurd
Speaking a language of
Just one word?

by Mary O'Neill

Reader 2: The next poem is about an animal that has humps that store fat. It uses the fat when there is no food. Otherwise, it would be hungry.

Reader 1: Let's read this together, too.

There Was a Camel

There was a camel
Who had two humps.
He thought in his youth
They were wisdom bumps.
Then he learned
They were nothing but humps—
And ever since he's
Been in the dumps.

by Langston Hughes

Reader 2: Finally, here's a poem about how we should treat all animals, baby ones, junior ones, and old ones. I'll read the first two lines.

Reader 1: I'll read the last two lines.

Always Be Kind to Animals

Always be kind to animals,
Morning, noon, and night;
For animals have feelings too,
And furthermore, they bite.

by John Gardner

Write an Animal Poem

Write an animal poem. Try to use the words slippery and steer. Talk about how you might use repetition, rhyme, and rhythm in your poem.

Making Connections

Text to Self

Discuss Changing How does a penguin chick grow and change? Tell a partner about two ways you have changed since you started second grade.

Text to Text

Fiction or Nonfiction Is *Penguin Chick* fiction or nonfiction? Find a fiction book about penguins. With a small group, make a chart to show the differences between that book and *Penguin Chick*.

Text to World

Connect to Science Use reference books to find pictures and facts about a bird you like. Write two facts about it. Share what you found with a partner.

Grammar

What Is an Adjective? An **adjective** is a word that describes how something looks, tastes, or smells. An adjective can also describe how something sounds or how it feels to touch.

Academic Language

adjective

Looks	Tastes or Smells	Sounds	Feels
yellow	sweet	noisy	crunchy
big	rotten	quiet	warm
pretty	spicy	loud	hard

Turn and Talk **With a partner, read each sentence aloud. Name the adjective in each sentence.**

1. The penguin chick ate a tasty meal.

2. The birds flop against the white snow.

3. The egg sits on his webbed feet.

4. We heard loud singing.

Sentence Fluency Sometimes you may write two sentences with adjectives that tell about the same noun. Join the sentences, using **and** between the two adjectives. This will make your writing better.

Short, Choppy Sentences	
Penguin chicks are cute.	Penguin chicks are fuzzy.

Longer, Smoother Sentence

Penguin chicks are cute and fuzzy.

Connect Grammar to Writing

When you revise your problem-solution paragraph, try to combine sentences that have adjectives telling about the same noun.

Write to Inform

When you write to inform, use exact words to give your reader more information.

Matt drafted a **problem-solution paragraph** about how to solve a problem at his school. Later, he revised by adding some exact words.

Writing Traits Checklist

✓ Ideas
Did I clearly state the solution to the problem?

✓ Organization
Did I start by telling what the problem is?

✓ Word Choice
Did I use exact words?

✓ Conventions
Did I use resources to help me spell everything correctly?

Revised Draft

Our class has been studying penguins. Most of us have only
Where could we see live penguins?
seen penguins on television. ∧
The students in our class
∧ Some people voted on how to
problem
solve this ∧ thing. We can go on
to the aquarium
a field trip. ∧

214

Live Penguins
by Matt Knightley

Our class has been studying penguins. Most of us have only seen penguins on television. Where could we see live penguins? The students in our class voted on how to solve this problem. We can go on a field trip to the aquarium. They have a penguin exhibit there. This way we can see live penguins close up.

> I changed words and added words to give more information.

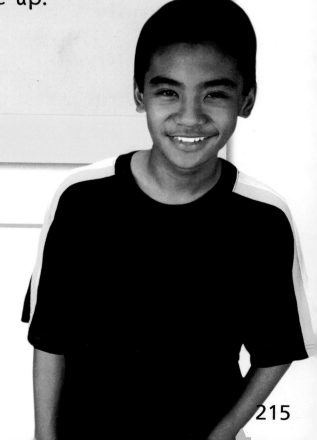

Reading as a Writer

Which exact words did Matt add to give the reader more information? Which exact words can you add to your writing?

215

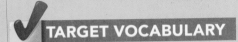
TARGET VOCABULARY

knot

copy

planning

lonely

heavily

seriously

answered

guessed

Vocabulary
Reader

Context
Cards

Vocabulary
in Context

● **Read each Context Card.**

● **Make up a new sentence
that uses one of the
Vocabulary words.**

1 **knot**
The boy showed how a
strong knot in a rope can
hold things together.

2 **copy**
You can copy the outline of
your hand by tracing over it
onto a chalkboard.

3 planning

They are **planning** to fly their kite at the park today.

4 lonely

She misses her friend who moved to another town. She is **lonely**.

5 heavily

It was raining **heavily**. The umbrella kept them from getting soaking wet.

6 seriously

The boy takes playing chess **seriously**. He does not laugh or joke around.

7 answered

When the phone rang, she **answered** it and said hello.

8 guessed

The boy hid his eyes. He **guessed** that his friend was hiding behind a big tree.

Background

Good Friends With a friend, you will never feel lonely. Haven't you smiled when a friend answered the phone? A friend will take what you say seriously. A friend who has guessed you are sad might tell a joke. A friend can help you in planning a party or untying a knot in your shoelace. A friend can help with a problem that weighs heavily on your mind. Friends might copy one another, but each is still special!

Comprehension

Understanding Characters

Julian is the main character in *Gloria Who Might Be My Best Friend*. He talks, acts, and thinks like a real person. Use a chart like this one to list details about Julian. Then use the details to figure out what Julian is like and why he acts the way he does.

Words	Actions	Thoughts

☑ TARGET STRATEGY **Question**

As you read, ask yourself questions. Ask why Julian and Gloria talk, act, think, and feel the way they do. Your questions and their answers will help you get to know the story characters better.

✔ TARGET VOCABULARY

knot	heavily
copy	seriously
planning	answered
lonely	guessed

✔ TARGET SKILL

Understanding Characters Tell more about characters.

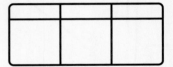

✔ TARGET STRATEGY

Question Ask questions about what you are reading.

GENRE

Realistic fiction is a story that could happen in real life.

MEET THE AUTHOR

ANN CAMERON

Sitting in a restaurant eating ice cream is Ann Cameron's favorite way to write. She has written many books about Julian and Gloria, including *Julian's Glorious Summer* and *Gloria's Way*.

MEET THE ILLUSTRATOR

MIKE REED

Mike Reed makes his home in Minnesota. There he teaches college art classes for students who want to learn how to use a computer to create artwork.

Gloria
Who Might Be My Best Friend

From THE STORIES JULIAN TELLS

by Ann Cameron   selection illustrated by Mike Reed

Essential Question

What can you learn from a character's words and actions?

221

If you have a girl for a friend, people find out and tease you. That's why I didn't want a girl for a friend—not until this summer, when I met Gloria.

It happened one afternoon when I was walking down the street by myself. My mother was visiting a friend of hers, and Huey was visiting a friend of his. Huey's friend is five and so I think he is too young to play with. And there aren't any kids just my age. I was walking down the street feeling lonely.

A block from our house I saw a moving van in front of a brown house, and men were carrying in chairs and tables and bookcases and boxes full of I don't know what. I watched for a while, and suddenly I heard a voice right behind me.

"Who are you?"

I turned around and there was a girl in a yellow dress. She looked the same age as me. She had curly hair that was braided into two pigtails with red ribbons at the ends.

"I'm Julian," I said. "Who are you?"

"I'm Gloria," she said. "I come from Newport. Do you know where Newport is?"

I wasn't sure, but I didn't tell Gloria. "It's a town on the ocean," I said.

"Right," Gloria said. "Can you turn a cartwheel?"

She turned sideways herself and did two cartwheels on the grass.

I had never tried a cartwheel before, but I tried to copy Gloria. My hands went down in the grass, my feet went up in the air, and—I fell over.

I looked at Gloria to see if she was laughing at me. If she was laughing at me, I was going to go home and forget about her.

But she just looked at me very seriously and said, "It takes practice," and then I liked her.

✔ STOP AND THINK

Understanding Characters
What do you learn about Gloria when Julian does a cartwheel?

"I know where there's a bird's nest in your yard,"
I said.

"Really?" Gloria said. "There weren't any trees in
the yard, or any birds, where I lived before."

I showed her where a robin lives and has eggs.
Gloria stood up on a branch and looked in. The
eggs were small and pale blue. The mother robin
squawked at us, and she and the father robin flew
around our heads.

"They want us to go away," Gloria said. She got down from the branch, and we went around to the front of the house and watched the moving men carry two rugs and a mirror inside.

"Would you like to come over to my house?" I said.

"All right," Gloria said, "if it is all right with my mother." She ran in the house and asked.

227

It was all right, so Gloria and I went to my house, and I showed her my room and my games and my rock collection, and then I made strawberry punch and we sat at the kitchen table and drank it.

"You have a red mustache on your mouth," Gloria said.

"You have a red mustache on your mouth, too," I said.

Gloria giggled, and we licked off the mustaches with our tongues.

"I wish you'd live here a long time," I told Gloria.

Gloria said, "I wish I would too."

"I know the best way to make wishes," Gloria said.

"What's that?" I asked.

"First you make a kite. Do you know how to make one?"

"Yes," I said, "I know how." I know how to make good kites because my father taught me. We make them out of two crossed sticks and folded newspaper.

"All right," Gloria said, "that's the first part of making wishes that come true. So let's make a kite."

We went out into the garage and spread out sticks and newspaper and made a kite. I fastened on the kite string and went to the closet and got rags for the tail.

"Do you have some paper and two pencils?" Gloria asked. "Because now we make the wishes."

I didn't know what she was planning, but I went in the house and got pencils and paper.

"All right," Gloria said. "Every wish you want to have come true you write on a long thin piece of paper. You don't tell me your wishes, and I don't tell you mine. If you tell, your wishes don't come true. Also, if you look at the other person's wishes, your wishes don't come true."

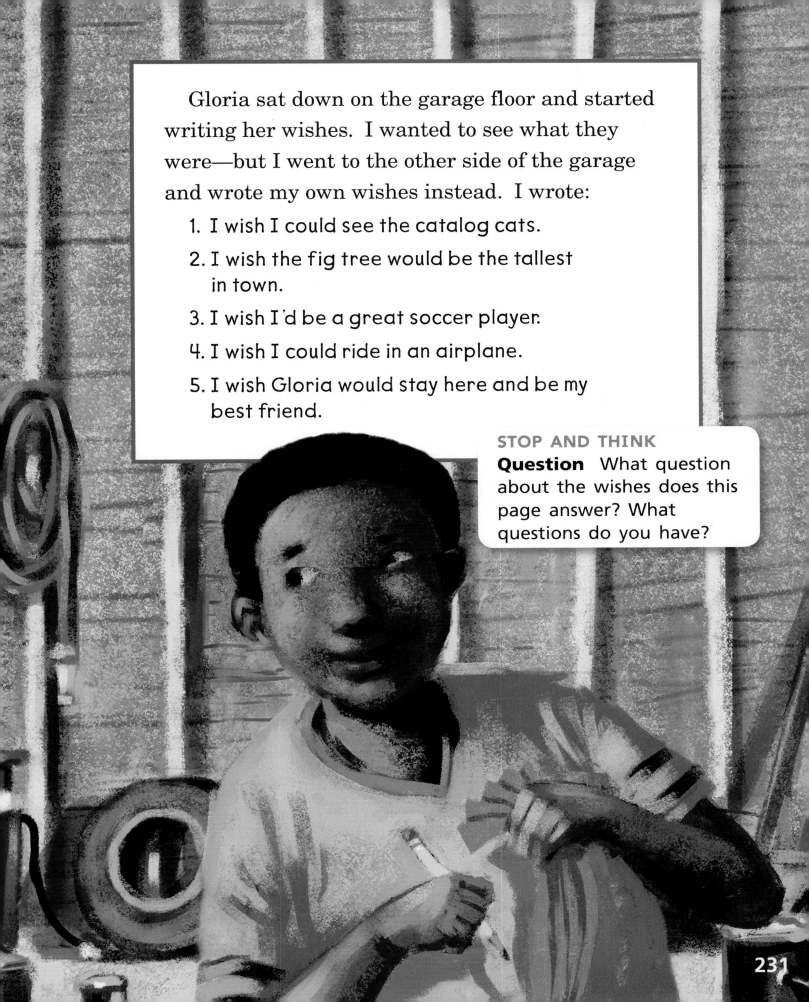

Gloria sat down on the garage floor and started writing her wishes. I wanted to see what they were—but I went to the other side of the garage and wrote my own wishes instead. I wrote:

1. I wish I could see the catalog cats.
2. I wish the fig tree would be the tallest in town.
3. I wish I'd be a great soccer player.
4. I wish I could ride in an airplane.
5. I wish Gloria would stay here and be my best friend.

STOP AND THINK

Question What question about the wishes does this page answer? What questions do you have?

231

I folded my five wishes in my fist and went over to Gloria.

"How many wishes did you make?" Gloria asked.

"Five," I said. "How many did you make?"

"Two," Gloria said.

I wondered what they were.

"Now we put the wishes on the tail of the kite," Gloria said. "Every time we tie one piece of rag on the tail, we fasten a wish in the knot. You can put yours in first."

I fastened mine in, and then Gloria fastened in hers, and we carried the kite into the yard.

"You hold the tail," I told Gloria, "and I'll pull."
We ran through the back yard with the kite, passed the garden and the fig tree, and went into the open field beyond our yard.

The kite started to rise. The tail jerked heavily like a long white snake. In a minute the kite passed the roof of my house and was climbing toward the sun.

STOP AND THINK

Author's Craft Why does the author describe the kite's tail as "like a long white snake"?

We stood in the open field, looking up at it. I was wishing I would get my wishes.

"I know it's going to work!" Gloria said.

"How do you know?"

"When we take the kite down," Gloria told me, "there shouldn't be one wish in the tail. When the wind takes all your wishes, that's when you know it's going to work."

The kite stayed up for a long time. We both held the string. The kite looked like a tiny black spot in the sun, and my neck got stiff from looking at it.

"Shall we pull it in?" I asked.

"All right," Gloria said.

We drew the string in more and more until, like a tired bird, the kite fell at our feet.

We looked at the tail. All our wishes were gone. Probably they were still flying higher and higher in the wind.

Maybe I would see the catalog cats and get to be a good soccer player and have a ride in an airplane and the tallest fig tree in town. And Gloria would be my best friend.

"Gloria," I said, "did you wish we would be friends?"

"You're not supposed to ask me that!" Gloria said.

"I'm sorry," I answered. But inside I was smiling. I guessed one thing Gloria wished for. I was pretty sure we would be friends.

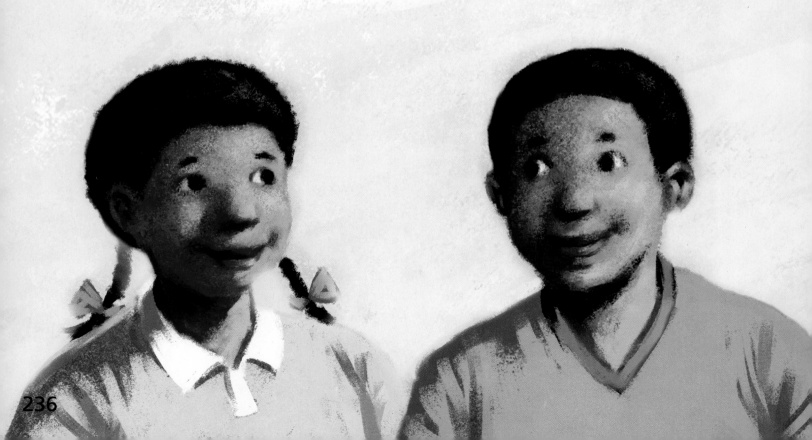

Your Turn

Pal Portrait

Write a Caption
Think of a friend that you like in the way that Julian likes Gloria. Draw a picture of your friend. Then write a caption for your picture. Tell why your friend is special. PERSONAL RESPONSE

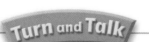 ## Words and Actions

Read the last page of the story again. What do you learn about Julian from his words and actions? Would you like to have Julian for a friend? Why or why not? Explain your ideas to a partner. UNDERSTANDING CHARACTERS

How to Make a Kite

by Joanna Korba

Can you feel lonely flying a kite? If you answered no, you guessed right!

If you take kite flying seriously, you will want to make your own kite. The first step in planning your kite is to read all of these directions. You may want to copy them onto another sheet of paper first.

Directions

Materials

2 sticks with small cuts on both ends

24 inches

18 inches

string

colored paper

glue and scissors

5 pieces of ribbon

What to Do

1 First, make a cross with the sticks. Tie a string around the middle.

2 Run string around the edge to make a frame. Tie it tightly at the top end. Then cut the string.

3 Lay the kite frame on the paper. Cut the paper so that it is slightly larger than the kite frame.

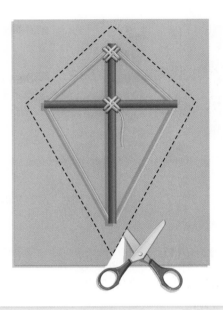

4 Fold the paper over the kite frame. Glue it down. Then tie a long string to the middle of the frame.

5 Cut a piece of string 36 inches long and make the tail. Tie a ribbon to the string every 6 inches with a tight knot. Too many ribbons will make your kite fly heavily.

Making Connections

 Text to Self

Tell About Making Friends What does Julian do to make Gloria his friend? What do you think makes a good friend? Explain.

 Text to Text

Compare Friendships Think about the friendships in *Dex: The Heart of a Hero* (Lesson 20) and *Gloria Who Might Be My Best Friend*. Make a chart to compare the friendships. What is the same and different?

Julian	Dex

 Text to World

Connect to Social Studies Julian and Gloria make a kite. Think of something you know how to make. Tell the directions to a partner. Have your partner retell and act out the directions.

Grammar

Using Adjectives Add *-er* to **adjectives** to compare two people, animals, places, or things. Add *-est* to compare more than two people, animals, places, or things.

Academic Language

adjectives

Comparing Two	Comparing More than Two
Lee is taller than Kim.	Lee is the tallest boy in class.
Maine is smaller than Texas.	Rhode Island is the smallest state.

Turn and Talk **Work with a partner to choose the correct adjective for each sentence. Then read the sentences aloud.**

1 I am (older, oldest) than my friend.

2 Main Street is the (longer, longest) street in town.

3 A kite flies (higher, highest) than a paper plane.

4 Gloria can do the (faster, fastest) cartwheels of all.

Ideas In your writing, use adjectives that compare to tell more about nouns. Add *-er* or *-est* to adjectives to compare two or more people, animals, places, or things.

Sentence That Does Not Tell Enough

Florian has a new kite.

Sentences That Tell More

Florian has a newer kite than Meg has.
Florian has the newest kite on the block.

✏ Connect Grammar to Writing

When you revise your paragraphs that compare and contrast, add *-er* or *-est* to adjectives to tell your reader more.

Write to Inform

When you write to **compare and contrast**, connect details to the main idea.

Leo wrote a draft to compare and contrast himself with his cousin. Later, he revised his draft to be sure his details connect to the main idea.

Writing Traits Checklist

✓ **Ideas**
Did I show ways in which people can be different?

✓ **Organization**
Do the details in each paragraph connect to the main idea?

✓ **Conventions**
Did I use spelling patterns and rules to spell words correctly?

✓ **Sentence Fluency**
Did I use transition words?

Revised Draft

My cousin Anthony and I are like twins. We are both the same age. We are about the same height. Anthony wears glasses, but I don't. I love scary movies, and so does he. We both like writing stories.

Even though we are alike in many ways, we are also different.

244

My Cousin and I
by Leo Saint-Clair

My cousin Anthony and I are like twins. We are both the same age. We are about the same height. I love scary movies, and so does he. We both like writing stories.

Even though we are alike in many ways, we are also different. Anthony wears glasses, but I don't. He's a great swimmer. I play chess. He loves loud music, and I love animals.

> I put details in one paragraph to compare, and details in the other to contrast.

Reading as a Writer

What did Leo move to make sure his details connect to the paragraph's main idea? Are your details in the right paragraph?

245

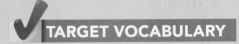
✓ TARGET VOCABULARY

yarn

strands

spinning

dye

weave

sharpening

duplicated

delicious

Vocabulary
Reader

Context
Cards

Vocabulary in Context

● Read each **Context Card**.

● Talk about a picture. Use a different Vocabulary word from the one on the card.

1
yarn
People use yarn to knit sweaters, hats, and mittens.

2
strands
The strands of yarn are tied into knots at the bottom of this rug.

246

3 spinning

It takes a lot of practice spinning chunks of wool into thin yarn.

4 dye

These shirts are soaked in dye to make them colorful.

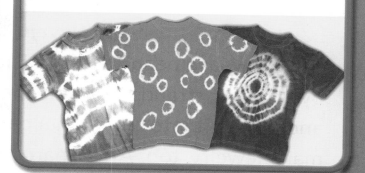

5 weave

This woman will weave dried grasses into baskets.

6 sharpening

This pencil does not need sharpening anymore!

7 duplicated

Some colors on this rug are duplicated. They appear again and again.

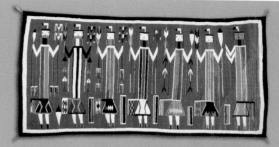

8 delicious

This baker makes delicious cakes. They are very tasty!

Background

Navajo Traditions Some Navajo people weave beautiful rugs. First, they make yarn by spinning strands of wool. Then they dye the yarn and weave it into traditional patterns. Many Navajo make jewelry, too. After sharpening their tools, they make jewelry of silver. The Navajo also make delicious traditional stews.

A handwoven rug like this cannot be duplicated.

This woman is weaving on an upright loom.

Comprehension

✔ TARGET SKILL **Conclusions**

In *The Goat in the Rug*, the authors don't say who Geraldine is. They only give story details as clues. As you read, use story details to help you draw conclusions about Geraldine and about making Navajo rugs. On a chart like this, write a conclusion and the story details you used to draw it.

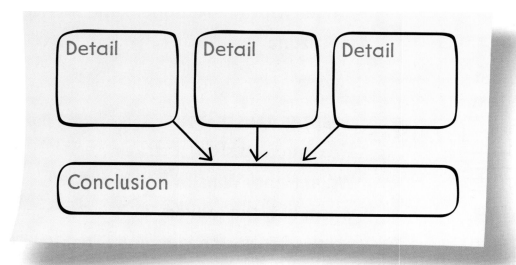

✔ TARGET STRATEGY **Summarize**

Use the conclusions you drew from story details in *The Goat in the Rug* to help you summarize important parts of the story.

TARGET VOCABULARY

yarn	weave
strands	sharpening
spinning	duplicated
dye	delicious

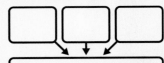
TARGET SKILL

Conclusions Use details to figure out more about the text.

TARGET STRATEGY

Summarize Stop to tell important ideas as you read.

Genre
Narrative Nonfiction tells a true story about a topic.

MEET THE AUTHORS

Charles L. Blood and Martin Link

These two authors wrote *The Goat in the Rug* from the point of view of Geraldine, the goat. Charles L. Blood also wrote a book about Native American crafts and games. Martin Link was once a ranger with the National Park Service in Arizona.

MEET THE ILLUSTRATOR

Nancy Winslow Parker

When Nancy Winslow Parker was a kid, she looked forward to spring cleaning. That was when her mom put new shelf paper in the kitchen cabinets and dresser drawers, and the young artist was given all the old paper to draw on.

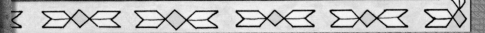

THE GOAT IN THE RUG

BY GERALDINE

as told to Charles L. Blood and Martin Link
illustrated by Nancy Winslow Parker

Essential Question

What helps you make a decision about a character?

My name is Geraldine and I live near a place called Window Rock with my Navajo friend, Glenmae. It's called Window Rock because it has a big round hole in it that looks like a window open to the sky.

Glenmae is called Glenmae most of the time because it's easier to say than her Indian name: Glee 'Nasbah. In English that means something like female warrior, but she's really a Navajo weaver. I guess that's why, one day, she decided to weave me into a rug.

I remember it was a warm, sunny afternoon. Glenmae had spent most of the morning sharpening a large pair of scissors. I had no idea what she was going to use them for, but it didn't take me long to find out.

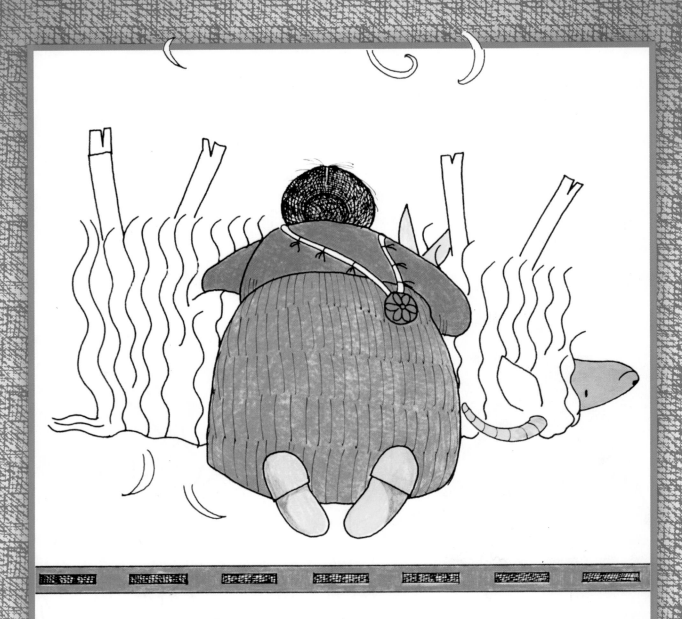

Before I knew what was happening, I was on the
ground and Glenmae was clipping off my wool in great
long strands. (It's called mohair, really.) It didn't hurt
at all, but I admit I kicked up my heels some. I'm very
ticklish for a goat.

I might have looked a little naked and silly
afterwards, but my, did I feel nice and cool! So I decided
to stick around and see what would happen next.

The first thing Glenmae did was chop up roots from a yucca plant. The roots made a soapy, rich lather when she mixed them with water.

She washed my wool in the suds until it was clean and white.

After that, a little bit of me (you might say) was hung up in the sun to dry. When my wool was dry, Glenmae took out two large square combs with many teeth.

By combing my wool between these carding combs, as they're called, she removed any bits of twigs or burrs and straightened out the fibers. She told me it helped make a smoother yarn for spinning.

STOP AND THINK

Summarize What has Glenmae done so far with Geraldine's wool?

Then, Glenmae carefully started to spin my wool—
one small bundle at a time—into yarn. I was beginning
to find out it takes a long while to make a Navajo rug.

Again and again, Glenmae twisted and pulled,
twisted and pulled the wool. Then she spun it around a
long, thin stick she called a spindle. As she twisted and
pulled and spun, the finer, stronger and smoother the
yarn became.

A few days later, Glenmae and I went for a walk. She said we were going to find some special plants she would use to make dye.

I didn't know what "dye" meant, but it sounded like a picnic to me. I do love to eat plants. That's what got me into trouble.

While Glenmae was out looking for more plants, I ate every one she had already collected in her bucket. Delicious!

The next day, Glenmae made me stay home
while she walked miles to a store. She said the dye
she could buy wasn't the same as the kind she makes
from plants, but since I'd made such a pig of myself, it
would have to do.

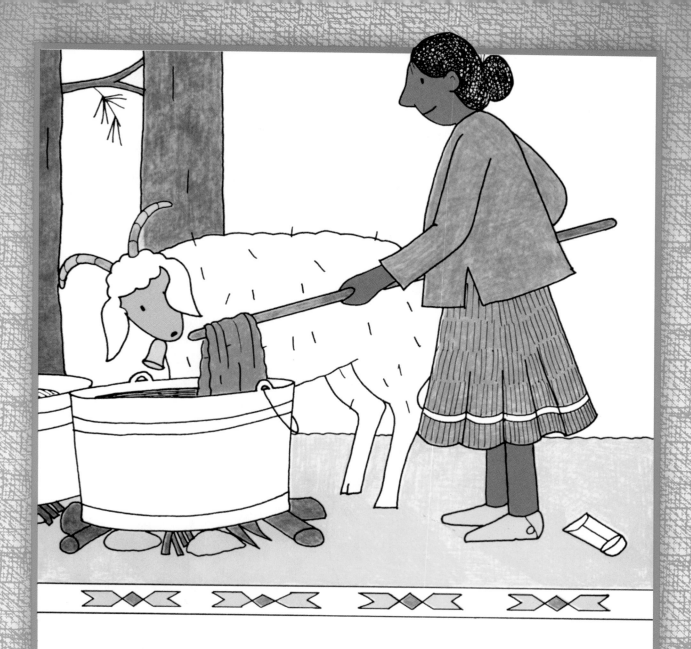

I was really worried that she would still be angry with me when she got back. She wasn't, though, and pretty soon she had three big potfuls of dye boiling over a fire.

Then I saw what Glenmae had meant by dyeing. She dipped my white wool into one pot . . . and it turned pink! She dipped it in again. It turned a darker pink! By the time she'd finished dipping it in and out and hung it up to dry, it was a beautiful deep red.

After that, she dyed some of my wool brown, and some of it black. I couldn't help wondering if those plants I'd eaten would turn all of me the same colors.

 STOP AND THINK

Conclusions Why does Geraldine think she'll turn red, brown, and black?

While I was worrying about that, Glenmae started to make our rug. She took a ball of yarn and wrapped it around and around two poles. I lost count when she'd reached three hundred wraps. I guess I was too busy thinking about what it would be like to be the only red, white, black, and brown goat at Window Rock.

It wasn't long before Glenmae had finished wrapping. Then she hung the poles with the yarn on a big wooden frame. It looked like a picture frame made of logs—she called it a "loom."

After a whole week of getting ready to weave, Glenmae started. She began weaving at the bottom of the loom. Then, one strand of yarn at a time, our rug started growing toward the top.

A few strands of black. A few of brown. A few of red. In and out. Back and forth. Until, in a few days, the pattern of our rug was clear to see.

Our rug grew very slowly. Just as every Navajo weaver before her had done for hundreds and hundreds of years, Glenmae formed a design that would never be duplicated.

STOP AND THINK
Author's Craft How do the words "A few, A few, A few, In and out, Back and forth" help you to feel what Glenmae is doing?

Then, at last, the weaving was finished! But not
until I'd checked it quite thoroughly in front and in back,
did I let Glenmae take our rug off the loom.

There was a lot of me in that rug. I wanted it to be perfect. And it was.

Since then, my wool has grown almost long enough for Glenmae and me to make another rug. I hope we do very soon. Because, you see, there aren't too many weavers like Glenmae left among the Navajos.

And there's only one goat like me, Geraldine.

This is the true story of a weaver and her goat who lived in the Navajo Nation at Window Rock, Arizona.

Your Turn

What Happens Next?

Write Directions

What steps did Glenmae take to make the rug? Draw each step. Then write the steps below the pictures. Make sure you summarize the steps. Use words like *first, next,* and *last* in your sentences to tell about the order of steps. SUMMARIZE

Turn and Talk Geraldine's Feelings

Do you think Geraldine likes spending time with Glenmae? What makes you think as you do? Share your ideas with a partner. Find examples from the story that support your ideas. CONCLUSIONS

269

Social Studies

GENRE

Informational text gives facts about a topic. This is a magazine article.

TEXT FOCUS

Photographs show true pictures of important details. **Captions** tell more information about a photo or picture. As you read, use captions and photos to help you.

Basket Weaving

by Becky Manfredini

A Texas Tradition

Texas Native Americans weave beautiful baskets. They make baskets in many shapes and sizes. Some are for storing delicious foods. Other baskets are to store clothes in. Some baskets are even used for carrying water! Basket makers make baskets for themselves and to sell.

Gathering Materials

Rug weavers have to make the material they use to weave rugs by spinning wool into yarn. Basket makers use strands of willow or special grasses to weave their baskets. After sharpening their cutting tools, basket makers go to places where the materials grow and cut off as much as they need.

Weaving is a tradition. Mothers teach their daughters how to weave.

How to Weave a Basket

Basket makers prepare the willow strands by soaking them in water. That makes them soft and easy to bend. It makes the strands much easier to weave. Then they weave the strands into a pattern.

Basket makers use dye they make from plants to make their baskets colorful. No basket is just like any other basket. The patterns are never duplicated. It takes a lot of skill to weave a beautiful basket.

The weaver holds thin strips of willow tightly as she works on this type of basket.

Making Connections

 Text to Self

Discuss a Skill What tools does Glenmae use to make the rug? Think of something you know how to do. Explain to a partner the tools you need for your skill and how to use them.

 Text to Text

Fact or Fiction Both "Basket Weaving" and *The Goat in the Rug* give facts about weaving. Which also contains made-up events? How do you know?

 Text to World

Connect to Social Studies Today many rugs are made by machines instead of by hand. Research some other things people used to make by hand.

Grammar

Irregular Verbs The **verbs** *have* and *has* can be used to tell what someone has right now. The verb *had* can be used to tell what someone had in the past. The verbs *do* and *does* can be used to tell what someone does right now. The verb *did* can be used to tell what someone did in the past.

Academic Language

verbs

Now	In the Past
I have a goat. She has a goat.	I had a goat when I was young. She had a goat a year ago.
We do nice work. He does nice work.	We did nice work yesterday. He did nice work last week.

Try This! **Choose the correct verb to complete each sentence. Then write the sentence correctly.**

❶ He (has, had) a loom now.

❷ I (do, did) many crafts last year.

❸ They (has, had) yarn before.

274

Conventions When you write, make sure you use the right form for the verbs in your sentences. The verb should match the subject of the sentence.

Wrong	Right
My uncle **have** many rugs in his store.	My uncle **has** many rugs in his store.
Last month, I **does** some work for him.	Last month, I **did** some work for him.

Connect Grammar to Writing

When you edit your writing, check to see if you have used the correct form for each verb.

Write to Inform

When you write, try not to repeat the same word too many times. Use synonyms instead. Synonyms are words that mean the same thing.

Kenny wrote an **informational paragraph** telling how Glenmae weaves a rug. Later Kenny revised his draft by replacing some of the words that repeated with synonyms.

Writing Traits Checklist

✔ **Ideas**
Did I include important information?

✔ **Organization**
Did I tell the steps in order?

✔ **Word Choice**
Did I use synonyms to avoid repeating words?

✔ **Conventions**
Did I capitalize and punctuate my sentences correctly?

Revised Draft

Glenmae has a special way of making yarn. First, she cuts the wool. She ^clips ~~cuts~~ off her goat's hair using scissors. Then she ^chops ~~cuts~~ up roots from a yucca plant.

How Glenmae Makes Yarn

By Kenny Hutchins

Glenmae has a special way of making yarn. First, she cuts the wool. She clips off her goat's hair using scissors. Then she chops up roots from a yucca plant. She mixes the roots with water. She uses this to wash the goat's hair. When the hair is dry, she uses two combs to straighten it. Then she twists and pulls the wool around a spindle. She does this many times until strong yarn is made.

In my final paper, I replaced some repeated words with synonyms.

Reading as a Writer

How did using many different words make Kenny's writing better? Where can you replace words with synonyms in your own paper?

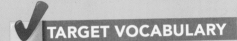
✓ **TARGET VOCABULARY**

tumbling

flung

tangled

empty

swift

peacefully

stream

blazed

Vocabulary
Reader

Context
Cards

Vocabulary in Context

● Study each **Context Card**.

● Ask a question that uses one of the Vocabulary words.

1
tumbling
This acrobat is tumbling through the air.

2
flung
When something is flung, it is thrown with force.

3 tangled

These pieces of string are tangled. It is hard to separate them.

4 empty

This pot is empty. There is nothing in it.

5 swift

Swift horses move very fast.

6 peacefully

The farm animals are sleeping peacefully. Nothing is bothering them.

7 stream

This stream flows into a larger river.

8 blazed

A forest fire blazed, or burned brightly, for many hours.

279

Background

✓ TARGET VOCABULARY   **Fantastic Folktales** People have been telling folktales for many, many years. Folktales often have events that could not happen in real life. Stars may be flung into the sky. A sun that blazed above may come tumbling down. In a folktale, a swift wind can get tangled in the trees. A chicken and a stream may talk to each other. Amazing things can happen, such as gold appearing in an empty pot. Folktales usually end peacefully.

Comprehension

✔ **TARGET SKILL**   Cause and Effect

In *Half-Chicken*, some events cause other events to happen. The first event is the cause. The second event is the effect. Use a chart like this one as you read to list some causes and effects in the story.

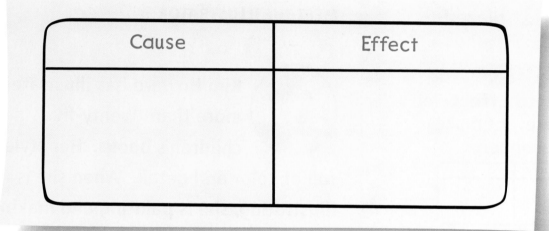

Cause	Effect

✔ **TARGET STRATEGY**   Visualize

Use the story details about causes and effects to visualize what happens to Half-Chicken. Look for words and phrases that help you create pictures in your mind.

✔ TARGET VOCABULARY

tumbling	swift
flung	peacefully
tangled	stream
empty	blazed

✔ TARGET SKILL

Cause and Effect Tell how one event makes another happen.

✔ TARGET STRATEGY

Visualize Picture what is happening as you read.

GENRE
A **folktale** is a story that is often told by people of a country.

MEET THE AUTHOR
Alma Flor Ada

Alma Flor Ada comes from a family of storytellers. She first heard the story of Half-Chicken from her grandmother. It was one of her favorites as a child. She loved the folktale so much that she decided to write her own retelling of it.

MEET THE ILLUSTRATOR
Kim Howard

Kim Howard has illustrated more than twenty-five children's books. Her style is full of color and detail. When she is not illustrating, she is painting and making collages. She also teaches students all over the world about art.

HALF-CHICKEN

by Alma Flor Ada
illustrated by Kim Howard

Essential Question

How can one event in a story cause another to happen?

283

Have you ever seen a weather vane? Do you know why there is a little rooster on one end, spinning around to let us know which way the wind is blowing?

Well, I'll tell you. It's an old, old story that my grandmother once told me. And before that, her grandmother told it to her. It goes like this . . .

A long, long time ago, on a Mexican ranch, a mother hen was sitting on her eggs. One by one, the baby chicks began to hatch, leaving their empty shells behind. One, two, three, four . . . twelve chicks had hatched. But the last egg still had not cracked open.

The hen did not know what to do. The chicks were running here and there, and she could not chase after them because she was still sitting on the last egg.

Finally there was a tiny sound. The baby chick was pecking at its egg from the inside. The hen quickly helped it break open the shell, and at last the thirteenth chick came out into the world.

Yet this was no ordinary chick. He had only one wing, only one leg, only one eye, and only half as many feathers as the other chicks.

STOP AND THINK
Visualize What words does the author use to help you picture what the chick looks like?

286

It was not long before everyone at the ranch
knew that a very special chick had been born.
    The ducks told the turkeys. The turkeys told
the pigeons. The pigeons told the swallows. And
the swallows flew over the fields, spreading the
news to the cows grazing peacefully with their
calves, the fierce bulls and the swift horses.

Soon the hen was surrounded by animals who wanted to see the strange chick.

One of the ducks said, "But he only has one wing!"

And one of the turkeys added, "Why, he's only a . . . half chicken!"

From then on, everyone called him Half-Chicken. And Half-Chicken, finding himself at the center of all this attention, became very vain.

One day he overheard the swallows, who traveled a great deal, talking about him: "Not even at the court of the viceroy in Mexico City is there anyone so unique."

Then Half-Chicken decided that it was time for him to leave the ranch. Early one morning he said his farewells, announcing:

"Good-bye, good-bye!
I'm off to Mexico City
to see the court of the viceroy!"

And *hip hop hip hop*, off he went, hippety-hopping along on his only foot.

✔ STOP AND THINK
Cause and Effect Why does Half-Chicken decide to leave the ranch?

Half-Chicken had not walked very far when he found a stream whose waters were blocked by some branches.

"Good morning, Half-Chicken. Would you please move the branches that are blocking my way?" asked the stream.

Half-Chicken moved the branches aside. But when the stream suggested that he stay awhile and take a swim, he answered:

I have no time to lose.
I'm off to Mexico City
to see the court of the viceroy!"

And *hip hop hip hop*, off he went, hippety-hopping along on his only foot.

A little while later, Half-Chicken found a small fire burning between some rocks. The fire was almost out.

"Good morning, Half-Chicken. Please, fan me a little with your wing, for I am about to go out," asked the fire.

Half-Chicken fanned the fire with his wing, and it blazed up again. But when the fire suggested that he stay awhile and warm up, he answered:

"I have no time to lose.
I'm off to Mexico City
to see the court of the viceroy!"

And *hip hop hip hop*, off he went, hippety-hopping along on his only foot.

After he had walked a little farther, Half-Chicken found the wind tangled in some bushes.

"Good morning, Half-Chicken. Would you please untangle me, so that I can go on my way?" asked the wind.

Half-Chicken untangled the branches. But when the wind suggested that he stay and play, and offered to help him fly here and there like a dry leaf, he answered:

"I have no time to lose.
I'm off to Mexico City
to see the court of the viceroy!"

And *hip hop hip hop*, off he went, hippety-hopping along on his only foot. At last he reached Mexico City.

Half-Chicken crossed the enormous Great Plaza. He passed the stalls laden with meat, fish, vegetables, fruit, cheese, and honey. He passed the Parián, the market where all kinds of beautiful goods were sold. Finally, he reached the gate of the viceroy's palace.

STOP AND THINK
Author's Craft The author repeats the same phrase throughout the story. Why does the author do this?

293

"Good afternoon," said Half-Chicken to the guards in fancy uniforms who stood in front of the palace. "I've come to see the viceroy."

One of the guards began to laugh. The other one said, "You'd better go in around the back and through the kitchen."

So Half-Chicken went, *hip hop hip hop*, around the palace and to the kitchen door.

The cook who saw him said, "What luck! This chicken is just what I need to make a soup for the vicereine." And he threw Half-Chicken into a kettle of water that was sitting on the fire.

When Half-Chicken felt how hot the water was, he said, "Oh fire, help me! Please, don't burn me!"

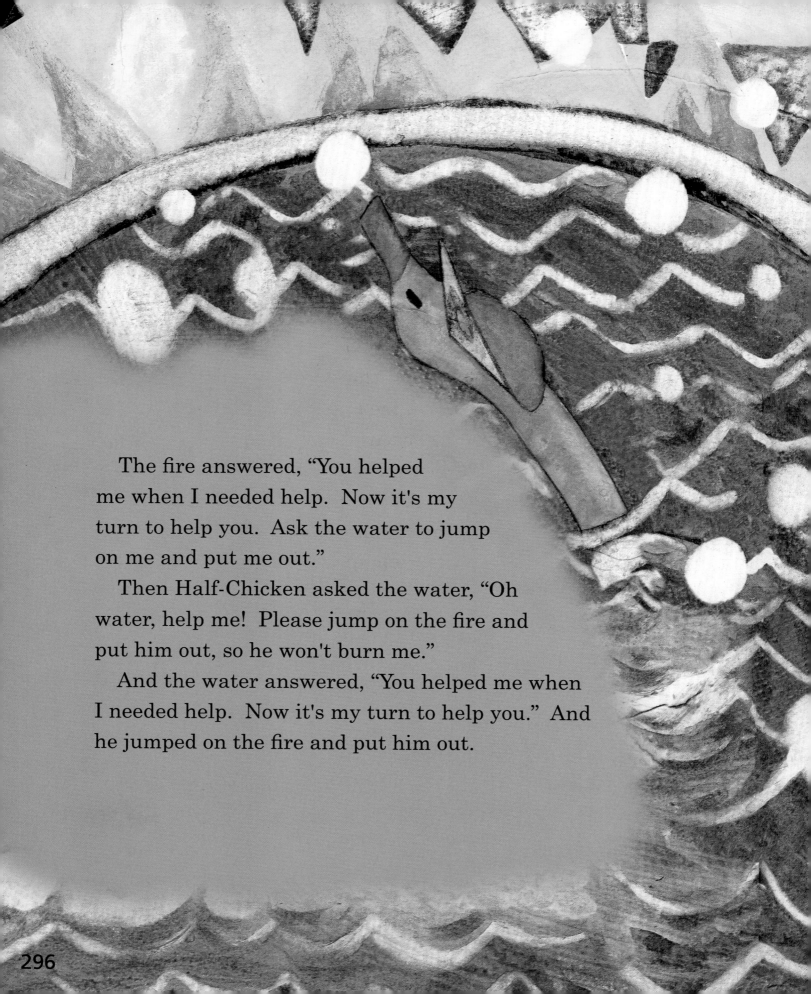

The fire answered, "You helped me when I needed help. Now it's my turn to help you. Ask the water to jump on me and put me out."

Then Half-Chicken asked the water, "Oh water, help me! Please jump on the fire and put him out, so he won't burn me."

And the water answered, "You helped me when I needed help. Now it's my turn to help you." And he jumped on the fire and put him out.

When the cook returned, he saw that the water had spilled and the fire was out.

"This chicken has been more trouble than he's worth!" exclaimed the cook. "Besides, one of the ladies-in-waiting just told me that the vicereine doesn't want any soup. She wants to eat nothing but salad."

And he picked Half-Chicken up by his only leg and flung him out the window.

When Half-Chicken was tumbling through the air, he called out: "Oh wind, help me, please!"

And the wind answered, "You helped me when I needed help. Now it's my turn to help you."

And the wind blew fiercely. He lifted Half-Chicken higher and higher, until the little rooster landed on one of the towers of the palace.

"From there you can see everything you want, Half-Chicken, with no danger of ending up in the cooking pot."

And from that day on, weathercocks have stood on their only leg, seeing everything that happens below, and pointing whichever way their friend the wind blows.

Your Turn

Helping Out

Write to Explain

Half-Chicken was very vain. However, he also showed that he could be thoughtful of others. Think of the ways in which Half-Chicken was thoughtful and helpful. Write a paragraph to explain. Use examples from the story. UNDERSTANDING CHARACTERS

Turn and Talk — Different Endings

What might have happened if the fire, water, and wind had not helped Half-Chicken at the end of the story? How would the story have ended differently? Talk about your ideas with a partner. CAUSE AND EFFECT

The Lion and the Mouse

Once a lion was sleeping peacefully in the grass. Then a mouse ran up his tail. The lion woke up. He grabbed the mouse and flung it. The mouse went tumbling across the ground.

"Please don't eat me," the mouse cried. "I promise that I will help you one day if you let me go."

"You help me?" the lion laughed. "I will let you go because you are so funny!"

Later, the lion was having a drink at a stream. He saw that a campfire blazed across the way. The camp was empty.

"Hunters must be near," he said. Just then a net fell on him. The lion was tangled in it. He roared with all his might.

Suddenly, the mouse appeared. "I will get you out in no time."

The swift mouse nibbled at the net. Soon, the lion was free.

"I didn't believe you could help me," said the lion. "You saved my life."

"It was simply my turn to help you," said the mouse.

MORAL: Little friends can turn out to be great friends.

Making Connections

 Text to Self

Tell a Moral Story Think about the morals of *Half-Chicken* and *The Lion and the Mouse*. When have you helped someone? Tell a partner the story of what happened.

 Text to Text

Compare and Contrast Write a paragraph that tells how *Half-Chicken* and *The Lion and the Mouse* are alike and different. Compare their settings, characters, and plots.

 Text to World

Connect to Art Work with a small group to design your own weather vane, using an animal other than a chicken. Draw a plan that shows what the weather vane would look like.

Grammar

Irregular Action Verbs The **verbs** *run, come, see,* and *go* name an action that is happening now. Do not add *-ed* to these verbs to tell what happened in the past. Instead use *ran, came, saw,* and *went.*

What Is Happening Now	What Happened in the Past
I run down the road.	I ran down the road yesterday.
People come to the farm to look at the chicken.	People came to the farm to look at the chicken last fall.
They see the wind blowing.	Yesterday, they saw the wind blowing.
We go to the plaza.	We went to the plaza last year.

Turn and Talk **Read each sentence aloud. Change each underlined verb to tell what happened in the past. Read the new sentences. Stay on topic as you work.**

1. I run past a farm with a weather vane.

2. I come back for my friend Mike.

3. We see the chicken.

4. The weather vanes go around and around.

304

Word Choice When you write, use exact verbs. They make your sentences interesting and tell your reader more about what is happening.

Without Exact Verb	With Exact Verb
The chicken **went** down the road.	The chicken **tumbled** down the road.

Verb	Exact Verbs
run	race, zoom, dash, speed
see	spot, watch, sight, spy
go	move, chase, leave, flee
come	near, enter, reach, arrive

Connect Grammar to Writing

When you revise your research report next week, look for any verbs that you can change to more exact verbs.

Write to Inform

☑ **Ideas** When you write a **research report,** you can use a K-W-L chart to help you plan your writing.

Rosa started with a K-W-L chart on giraffes. She made notes about what she learned. She added more details. Finally, she put the information in order.

Writing Process Checklist

▶ **Prewrite**

☑ **Did I choose an interesting topic?**

☑ **Did I do research to answer my question?**

☑ **Did I come up with details that will inform the reader about my topic?**

Draft

Revise

Edit

Publish and Share

Exploring a Topic

What I Know	What I Want to Know	What I Learned
Giraffes are wild animals.	Where they live	Grasslands of Africa
Giraffes are tall.	How tall are they?	Tallest animals 18 feet
They have long necks.	What do they eat?	Eat acacia leaves Get water from leaves

Flow Chart

Giraffes live on the grasslands of Africa.

↓

They are 18 feet tall with long necks, spots, hairy horns.

↓

They eat acacia leaves, which also give them water.

↓

Lions, crocodiles, hyenas, wild dogs are their enemies.

↓

Giraffes stay together, watch for enemies, and are fast.

I put the information I learned in an order that makes sense.

Reading as a Writer

What did Rosa add to her K-W-L chart?
How did she organize her information?
How will you organize your information?

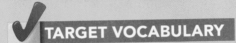
✓ TARGET VOCABULARY

crops

sprouting

blossomed

drooping

underneath

harmful

fortunate

promised

Vocabulary Reader

Context Cards

Vocabulary in Context

- Read each **Context Card**.
- Place the Vocabulary words in alphabetical order.

1 crops

A farmer grows crops, such as squash, tomatoes, carrots, and corn.

2 sprouting

The plants in the garden are sprouting, or starting to grow.

3 blossomed

The apple trees have just **blossomed**. The flowers will turn into fruit.

4 drooping

A **drooping** plant would need some water on a hot day.

5 underneath

On a sunny day, a toad keeps cool by sitting **underneath** a leaf.

6 harmful

This bug is **harmful** because it eats vegetables and other plants.

7 fortunate

This farmer is **fortunate**, or lucky, to have such a good crop of tomatoes.

8 promised

This girl **promised** to water the garden, and she did.

Background

Growing Seeds Some people grow crops of tomatoes. First, they plant seeds. Then they water them until they start sprouting. The sprouts push up, and the roots grow underneath the ground. If the sprouts start drooping, they need more water. Too much watering can be harmful. After the plants have blossomed, they produce tomatoes. A fortunate gardener is promised many delicious tomatoes!

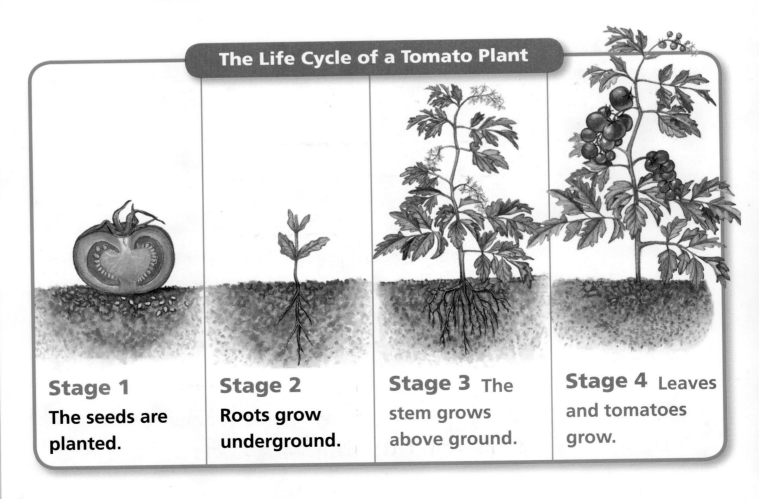

The Life Cycle of a Tomato Plant

Stage 1
The seeds are planted.

Stage 2
Roots grow underground.

Stage 3 The stem grows above ground.

Stage 4 Leaves and tomatoes grow.

Comprehension

✔ **TARGET SKILL** **Sequence of Events**

In *How Groundhog's Garden Grew,* Little Groundhog learns how to grow a garden. As you read, notice what he does first, next, and last. This will help you understand the sequence, or the order, of events. List the events in order on a chart like this one.

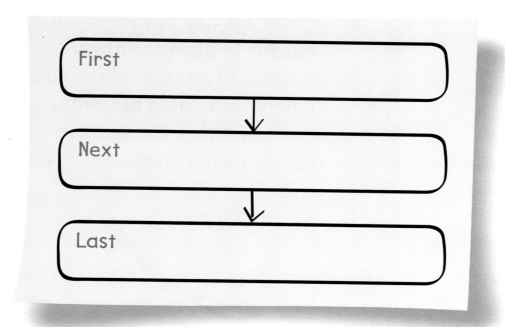

✔ **TARGET STRATEGY** **Monitor/Clarify**

Pay attention to the steps Little Groundhog follows to grow a garden. If a step does not make sense, reread the part or read ahead. Think of how the sequence can help you understand what Little Groundhog does.

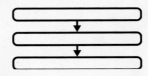

✔ **TARGET VOCABULARY**

crops	underneath
sprouting	harmful
blossomed	fortunate
drooping	promised

✔ **TARGET SKILL**
Sequence of Events
Tell the order in which things happen.

✔ **TARGET STRATEGY**
Monitor/Clarify Find ways to figure out what doesn't make sense.

GENRE
A **fantasy** is a story that could not happen in real life.

MEET THE AUTHOR AND ILLUSTRATOR
Lynne Cherry

Lynne Cherry has been growing her own vegetables ever since she was a little girl. Her parents taught her how to plant seeds, pull weeds, and take care of the soil.

Now Ms. Cherry tries to encourage students to plant their own gardens. At one school she visited, students presented her with a giant cauliflower they had grown after reading *How Groundhog's Garden Grew!*

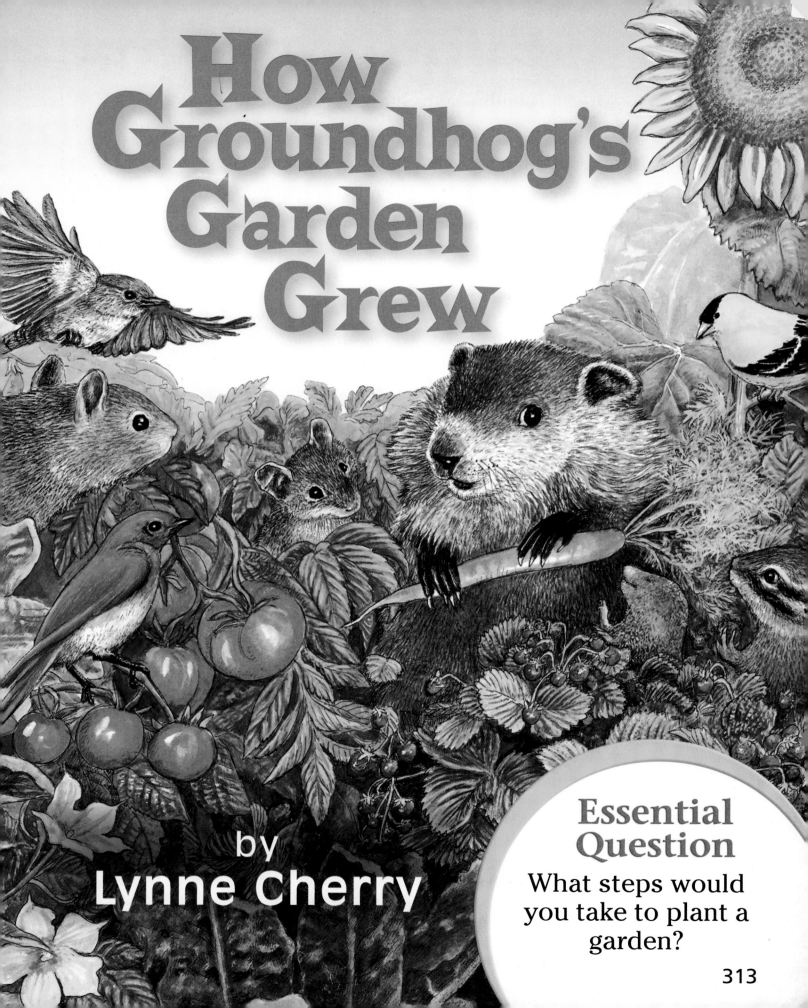

How Groundhog's Garden Grew

by
Lynne Cherry

Essential Question

What steps would you take to plant a garden?

Little Groundhog was hungry. "Beautiful! Scrumptious! Irresistible!" he exclaimed as he crept into a neighbor's lovely vegetable garden. He was nibbling on some fresh green lettuce when Squirrel rushed down from her tree.

"Little Groundhog!" Squirrel scolded. "This food does not belong to you. If you take food that belongs to others, you will not have a friend in the world! Why don't you plant your OWN garden?"

"I'm sorry," Little Groundhog told her, embarrassed, "but I don't know how."

"Well, then," replied Squirrel, "I will show you."

onion sets

Lima beans

cantaloupe

radish

sweet
pepper
seeds

"First, you will need seeds," said Squirrel.
Little Groundhog helped Squirrel and
her friends pick beans and peas from
pods, and seeds from a sunflower's
drooping head.

squash seeds

Lima beans

sunflower seeds

peas

asparagus
seeds

They collected seeds from inside peppers, cantaloupes, cucumbers, and tomatoes.

Squirrel chewed a hole into a pumpkin and handed Little Groundhog the gooey seeds, saying, "We'll dry these in the sun. Then we can plant them in the spring!"

✔ **STOP AND THINK**

Sequence of Events What is the first thing Squirrel showed Groundhog about planting his own garden?

pumpkin
seeds

bell pepper
seeds

317

A chill breeze blew in. "It's time to dig up potatoes," Squirrel said. Little Groundhog watched Squirrel and thought, "That looks like fun!" and so he took a rake and poked around for potatoes, too. When they were finished, Squirrel added composted leaves to her garden as fertilizer for the coming year.

Squirrel put aside a few potatoes and the tops of onions in a burlap sack. She put the seeds they had collected in tins to keep them dry and put the tins into her sack.

November's snow flurries told Squirrel that winter was on its way.

"Sweet dreams, Little Groundhog," Squirrel said as she curled up in her tree hole.

"See you in the spring," Little Groundhog said, snuggling into his deep earthen burrow. As winter snows blew, Little Groundhog and Squirrel slept.

In February, Little Groundhog awoke and drowsily ambled up to the burrow entrance. The wind made him shiver. He saw his shadow and hurried back inside.

"Oh my," he said. "This will be a long winter."

Weeks later, he awoke with a start. "It's spring!" he shouted, and up he scuttled to the burrow entrance. There he met Squirrel carrying the burlap sack they had filled with potatoes and the tins of seeds.

"Rise and shine!" Squirrel said. "It's planting time! Look! The potatoes are sprouting!"

"First, we'll cut them into little pieces with two sprouts each. Then, we'll plant them with their sprouts pointing up and cover them with soil. Each sprout will grow into a new potato plant. Next fall, we'll dig new potatoes out of the ground. Now let's find a sunny place for your garden!"

> **STOP AND THINK**
> **Monitor/Clarify** What has happened to the potatoes that were in the sack all winter?

When they found a good spot, Squirrel told Little Groundhog, "First, we need to dig in the soil to loosen it up." Next, they planted the cut-up potatoes. Then, they dug rows and sprinkled in carrot, beet, parsnip, and radish seeds.

"All these vegetables will grow under the ground," Squirrel told him, "so we call them root crops."

They covered the seeds with dirt and gently watered them. At the end of each row, Squirrel stuck markers to help them remember what they had planted.

pole bean seeds

bell pepper seeds

mustard greens

mung beans

swiss chard

cantaloupe

peas

corn

Squirrel told Little Groundhog, "Plants need lots of sun. We'll plant taller vegetables in the back so they won't cast a shadow over the shorter ones."

So behind the rows of root crops, they planted seeds of tomatoes, peppers, and leafy greens.

cilantro

radish

lettuce

lettuce

lettuce

cut-up potato pieces

parsnip seeds

"Some vegetables grow on vines," said Squirrel. She pounded sticks into the ground for the pea and bean plants to climb.

"Some plants grow very big," said Squirrel. They planted the seeds of pumpkins, zucchini, yellow squash, sunflowers, corn, and artichokes far apart to give them lots of room to grow.

carrot seeds

tomato seeds

onion sets

sweet pepper seeds

eggplant seeds

pole snap bean

cucumber seeds

beet seeds

turnip seeds

The next day, Squirrel said, "Let's visit my garden. I want to show you the plants that come up year after year all by themselves. They're called perennials." Sure enough, shoots of raspberries and asparagus were already poking up through the ground.

Squirrel dug up a frilly young asparagus plant for Little Groundhog's garden. She told him, "You'll need to wait three years before this asparagus has nice, thick stems to eat."

Little Groundhog said, "Thank you! I'm off to plant my per-ren-ne-als."

Every day, Little Groundhog watched and waited and watered his garden. Then one day, tiny seedlings emerged. "What a wonder!" he exclaimed.

But as they grew, he worried. "Are these seedlings too crowded together? What should I do?" he asked Squirrel.

"Pull some up and plant them somewhere else," she said.

Little Groundhog pulled up a few seedlings and looked at them. The peas, the beans, and all the seeds had split open. From each, a root grew down and a shoot grew up. Little Groundhog transplanted some seedlings where they had more room to grow.

STOP AND THINK
Author's Craft
What do you learn from the things that Groundhog and Squirrel say to each other?

sunflower

325

strangalia

blueberry bee
osmia ribifloris

parasitic wasp

alfalfa
leaf-cutter bee

metallic
agapostemon
sweat bee

squash bee

longhorn bee

syrphid
flower fly

wren

Wren and Praying Mantis said to Little Groundhog, "If you promise not to harm us with bug spray, we birds and insects will help you with your garden. We will eat the harmful insects that hurt your plants." Little Groundhog promised.

As the weeks passed, plants grew and blossomed. Bees,

lightning bug
or firefly

firefly larvae

ladybug, ladybird
or beetle

cerotina

male halictid bee

green metallic bee

earthworm

bumble bee
bombus

female halictid
bee

green
metallic bee

ausoch
sweet b

326

rand
beetle

tiger
beetle

braconid
parasite

thread-waisted wasp

green
lacewing

Eastern
bluebird

flies, and butterflies came to eat the sweet
nectar and carried pollen from flower to flower. They
told Little Groundhog, "The wind, the rain, and we
insects pollinate your flowers so they can become
fruits and vegetables."

ladybug
larvae

ladybug,
ladybird,
or lady beetle

blue orchard
bee

megachile
leaf-
cutting bee

robin

carpenter bee
xylocopidae

apis
mellifera honeybee

andrena

ladybug, ladybird
or lady beetle

yellow squash

Little Groundhog noticed that after a flower was pollinated by an insect or by the wind, its petals dried up and fell off. Underneath was the smallest beginning of a tiny vegetable. . . .

"A tiny tomato! A tiny cucumber! A pepper! An eggplant! A pea pod! A zucchini! So this is how a garden grows!" Little Groundhog cried jubilantly.

snow peas

tomato

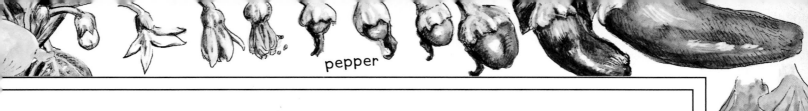
pepper

Tomatoes turned red. Heads of cabbage grew. A sunflower seemed to explode from the top of a tall stalk. Snap peas, string beans, peppers, lettuce, and chard grew larger under the warm sun. Little Groundhog rejoiced! He ate his very own vegetables, plain and fresh, from his very own garden all summer long.

eggplant

zucchini

329

When fall came again, Squirrel wanted to share one more secret with Little Groundhog—cooking. And so they stewed tomatoes, boiled corn, broiled potatoes, stir-fried veggies, and even stuffed and baked a zucchini, saving the seeds to plant the next year.

There was so much more than they could eat themselves.

"What do we do?" asked Little Groundhog.

"We share," said Squirrel.

"What a great idea!" cried Little Groundhog.

As they sat around the table, their friends exclaimed, "Thank you for inviting us to this amazing feast!"

Little Groundhog replied, "Thank you all for forgiving me for eating from your gardens last year. And thank you, Squirrel, for teaching me to grow my own! It's beautiful! Scrumptious! Irresistible! Let's eat!"

"What a fortunate creature I am," he thought. "Delicious, nutritious, homegrown food and wonderful friends to share it with."

Little Groundhog grew into a big groundhog and became known far and wide for his annual Thanksgiving dinner. And that is how Groundhog's garden grew!

Your Turn

 Teamwork

Puppet Show

Work with a partner to make stick puppets of Groundhog and Squirrel. Then use your puppets to show how Groundhog and Squirrel worked together to plant a garden. PARTNERS

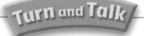 **Ready, Set, Grow!**

How did Groundhog and Squirrel plant their garden? Look through the story with a partner to find the steps that Groundhog and Squirrel took to plant their garden. Talk about what would have happened if they had not done the steps in order.
SEQUENCE OF EVENTS

✓ **TARGET VOCABULARY**

crops	underneath
sprouting	harmful
blossomed	fortunate
drooping	promised

GENRE

Informational text gives facts about a topic. This is a science text.

TEXT FOCUS

A **chart** is a drawing that lists information in a clear way.

SUPER SOIL

Soil contains many things. When insects, leaves, and twigs die and break down in the soil, they become humus. Tiny bits of broken rock are also found in soil. Soil holds water and air, too. The amount of humus, rock, air, and water in soil differs from place to place.

If someone promised to give you good soil for growing crops, what kind of soil would you be fortunate enough to get? Soil with lots of humus is best for growing crops.

All plants need water. They take water in through roots that grow underneath the ground. They need just the right amount of water for sprouting new growth. Too little water is harmful to plants and may cause drooping leaves.

Corn is an important crop in the United States. To grow, it needs soil with lots of humus.

Deserts are places that get little rain. There is not much humus in desert soil either. Most desert plants have shallow roots. The roots spread out just below the ground to catch rain water. Cactus plants store water in their stems. A creosote bush has waxy leaves that do not lose water in the hot sun. These plants grow well in dry desert soil. Many cactus plants have beautiful flowers. After the flowers have blossomed, they produce many tiny seeds.

Kinds of Soil

Topsoil	Clay Soil	Sandy Soil
• has a lot of humus. • is dark in color. • is best for plant growth.	• is made of tiny clay pieces. • is sticky when wet. • is brown, red, or yellow.	• has a lot of weathered rock. • feels gritty. • is tan or light brown.

Making Connections

Text to Self

Talk About Gardens What are some vegetables Groundhog grows? What vegetables would you like to grow? Share your ideas with a partner.

Text to Text

Connect to Poetry Groundhog's garden needed good soil to grow well. Read "Super Soil" again. Write a poem that tells how soil looks and feels and how it helps plants grow.

Good Soil, Good Food
Good, rich humus
and lots of rain
make my garden grow!

Text to World

List Celebrations At the end of the growing season, Groundhog shares a feast with friends. When else might people celebrate with their friends? Make a list, and circle your favorite event.

Grammar

More Irregular Action Verbs The **verbs** *say, eat, give,* and *take* tell what is happening now. Do not add *-ed* to these verbs to tell what happened in the past. Instead, use *said, ate, gave,* and *took.*

What Is Happening Now	What Happened in the Past
We say the plant names each day.	We said the plant names yesterday.
I eat beans this summer.	I ate beans last summer.
They always give vegetables to friends.	They gave vegetables to friends last night.
I take apples from a tree.	I took apples from a tree.

Turn and Talk **Work with a partner. Choose the correct verb for each sentence. Then read each sentence aloud.**

❶ I (taked, took) a pepper to make soup.

❷ We (ate, eaten) a harvest feast.

❸ She (gived, gave) me a tour of the garden.

❹ He (said, sayed) we could pick tomatoes.

Sentence Fluency When you write, make sure the verbs in your sentences all tell about the same time.

Incorrect: past, present

Yesterday, Kiley looked out her window.

She sees crows eating her corn.

Correct: past, past

Yesterday, Kiley looked out her window. She saw crows eating her corn.

Connect Grammar to Writing

When you revise your research report, check all the verbs to make sure they tell about the same time.

Write to Inform

☑ **Word Choice** When you write a **research report**, make sure you write the information and facts in your own words.

Rosa wrote a draft of her research report. Later, she revised her draft to put everything in her own words.

Writing Process Checklist

Prewrite

Draft

▶ **Revise**

☑ Do the details in each paragraph connect to the main idea?

☑ Did I use facts instead of opinions?

☑ Did I write the information I found in my research using my own words?

Edit

Publish and Share

Revised Draft

Giraffes are wild animals. They live in dry, grassy parts of Africa. Giraffes are the world's ~~The giraffe is the tallest~~ tallest animal! ~~mammal on Earth.~~ They grow to be about 18 feet tall. They have long necks and spots all over Two small horns grow their bodies. ~~They have two~~ on top of their heads. ~~distinct hair-covered horns.~~

Giraffes

by Rosa Marquez

Giraffes are wild animals. They live in dry, grassy parts of Africa.

Giraffes are the world's tallest animal! They grow to be about 18 feet tall. They have long necks and spots all over their bodies. Two small horns grow on top of their heads.

Giraffes eat the leaves of acacia trees. The water from these leaves helps them go for a long time without drinking.

> I revised my report so that all my information was in my own words.

Reading as a Writer

What did Rosa change to put the information in her own words? Is your writing in your own words?

Read the next two selections. Draw conclusions as you read.

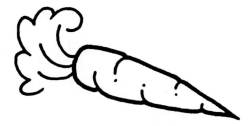

The Best Carrot

Farmer Rabbit adored carrots. He grew hundreds each year. However, he never shared a single one. One day Farmer Rabbit saw a huge carrot top. He pulled and pulled, but he could not get it out.

Bear saw Farmer Rabbit struggling. "I'll help you get that out if you give me half," he called.

"Not a chance!" said Farmer Rabbit.

Bear came by again later. The carrot was still stuck. "If you don't get that carrot out," said Bear, "it will rot. Is that really better than sharing it with me?"

Farmer Rabbit agreed to take Bear's offer. The carrot was the best Farmer Rabbit had tasted—even if he got only half.

Gardening Tips from the Green Thumb

This week's topic is *mulch*. I think mulch is the most important part of a garden. Mulch is anything used to cover the soil.

Some people use old leaves or grass to cover the soil. Others use bark or wood chips. Straw can make good mulch for a vegetable garden.

The best time to put down mulch is in the late spring. First, make sure you pull all the weeds in your garden. Then put the mulch on top of the soil, close to the plant.

Mulch can help your garden in many ways. When it is hot, the mulch helps keep water in the soil. When it is rainy, mulch keeps the soil from washing away. Mulch also helps keep the soil healthy, and it helps prevent weeds.

Unit 5 Wrap-Up

The Big Idea

Animals Grow and Change

All living things change as they grow. A chick becomes a penguin. A baby elephant becomes an adult. Choose an animal. Then write a picture story about how that animal might change as it grows.

Listening and Speaking

Sharing Stories Think about one of the animal stories in this unit. Then make a T-chart to help you tell a partner how that animal story is the same as and different from *Gloria, Who Might Be My Best Friend*.

Gloria, Who Might Be My Best Friend
and *The Goat in the Rug*

Same	Different
1. Two main characters	1. The goat tells one story. The boy tells the other story.

What a Surprise!

Unit 9

Big Idea

A surprise can change your life.

Paired Selections

Lesson

26

The Mysterious Tadpole
Fantasy
page 350

From Eggs to Frogs
Informational Text:
Science
page 372

Lesson

27

The Dog That Dug for Dinosaurs
Biography:
Science
page 384

La Brea Tar Pits
Informational Text:
Science
page 402

Lesson
28

Working in Space
Informational Text:
Science
page 414

Space Poems
Poetry
page 432

Lesson

29

Two of Everything
Folktale:
Traditional Tales
page 444

Stone Soup
Folktale:
Traditional Tales
page 462

Lesson

30

Now & Ben
Informational Text:
Social Studies
page 474

A Model Citizen
Informational Text:
Social Studies
page 494

✓ **TARGET VOCABULARY**
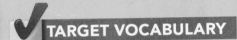

ordinary

control

cage

upset

sensible

confused

training

suspiciously

Vocabulary Reader   Context Cards

Vocabulary in Context

● Study each **Context Card**.

● Use a Vocabulary word to tell about something you did.

1   ordinary

An ostrich is not an **ordinary** bird. It runs quickly but cannot fly.

2   control

This rider uses reins to stay in **control** of the camel.

3 cage

If you own an iguana, you can let it out of its **cage**.

4 upset

This animal is **upset** because it sees danger.

5 sensible

These **sensible** hippos are smart enough to roll in cool mud on a hot day.

6 confused

This animal is not to be **confused** with a beaver or a duck. It's a platypus!

7 training

The **training** of a ferret takes time and patience.

8 suspiciously

The lemurs looked at the man **suspiciously**. They do not trust him.

Background

✓ TARGET VOCABULARY **Pet Care** Pets need water, food, and shelter. Birds and hamsters need a cage, while cats and dogs may sleep on an ordinary rug. If your pet gets sick or behaves suspiciously, you should take it to the vet. It is also sensible for you to keep your pet under control. Pets need proper training. They may become confused or upset when they don't know what you expect of them.

Pets depend on their owners to take good care of them.

348

Comprehension

Story Structure

Stories usually have characters, a setting, and a plot. Story details tell the reader about the characters, what is happening, and where the story takes place. Use a story map like this to keep track of the details in *The Mysterious Tadpole*.

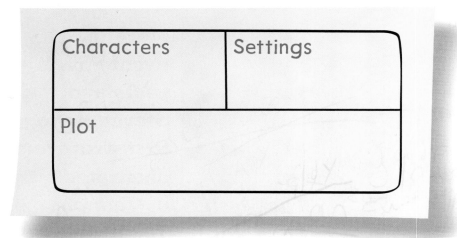

Characters	Settings
Plot	

✔ TARGET STRATEGY **Infer/Predict**

Is Alphonse really a tadpole? Use the information in your story map and what you already know to figure out more about him and his friend, Louis. Then make predictions about what will happen next. As you read, see if your predictions are correct.

Main Selection

✔ **TARGET VOCABULARY**

ordinary	sensible
control	confused
cage	training
upset	suspiciously

✔ **TARGET SKILL**

Story Structure Tell the setting, characters, and plot in a story.

✔ **TARGET STRATEGY**

Infer/Predict Use clues to figure out more about story parts.

GENRE

A **fantasy** is a story that could not happen in real life.

MEET THE AUTHOR AND ILLUSTRATOR

Steven Kellogg

More than twenty-five years ago, Steven Kellogg first wrote and illustrated *The Mysterious Tadpole.* Then, for the book's big anniversary, he published a new version with different illustrations and words. The new version is the one you are about to read.

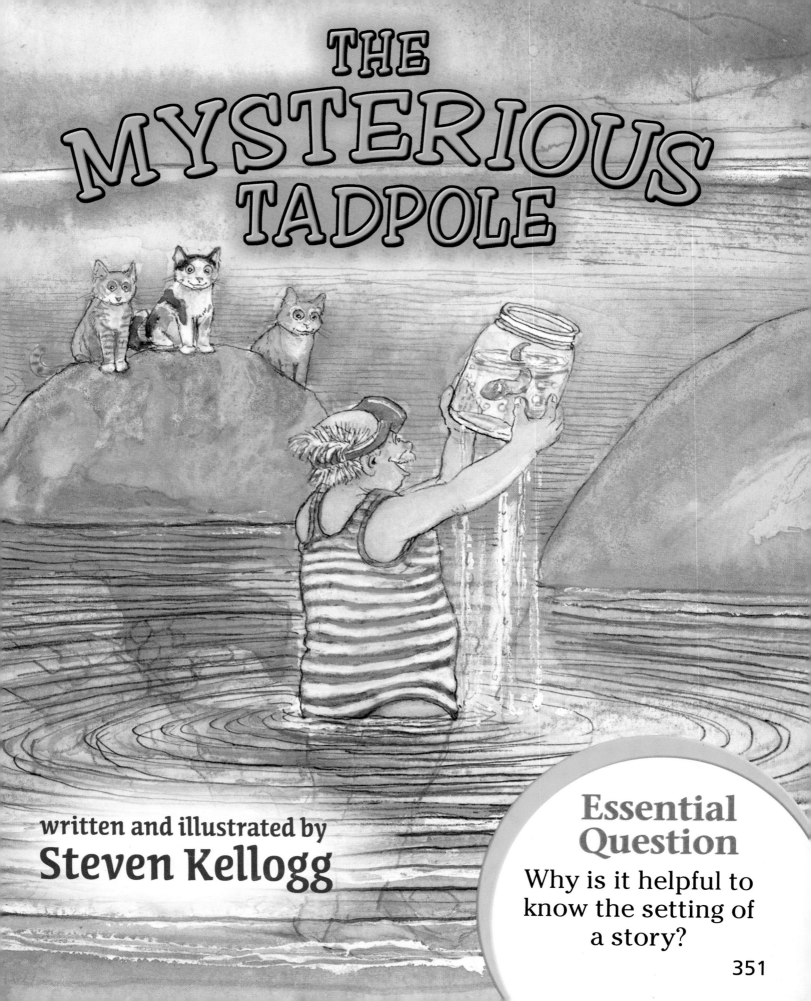

THE MYSTERIOUS TADPOLE

written and illustrated by
Steven Kellogg

Essential Question

Why is it helpful to know the setting of a story?

"Greetings, nephew!" cried Louis's uncle McAllister. "I've brought a wee bit of Scotland for your birthday."

"Thanks!" said Louis. "Look, Mom and Dad. It's a TADPOLE!"

Louis named him Alphonse and promised to take very good care of him.

Louis took Alphonse to school for show-and-tell.

"Class, here we have a splendid example of a tadpole," exclaimed Ms. Shelbert. "Let's ask Louis to bring it back every week so we can watch it become a frog."

Ms. Shelbert was amazed to see how quickly Alphonse grew.

"Maybe it's because he only eats cheeseburgers," said Louis.

When Alphonse became too big for his jar, Louis moved him to the kitchen sink. "He's the perfect pet!" said Louis.

Louis and Alphonse loved to play games.

"Be careful, Louis," said his mother. "The living room is not a soccer field. Something is going to get broken!"

And she was right. That same day the soccer ball slammed into Aunt Tabitha's antique lamp.

"This tadpole is out of control," said Louis's mother. "Something must be done."

"It won't happen again," promised Louis. "I'll take Alphonse to obedience school."

 **STOP AND THINK**
Story Structure Is Alphonse going to be a "perfect pet"? How can you tell?

354

The only animals at the obedience school were dogs.
Some of their owners stared at Alphonse suspiciously.
"Pretend you're a dog," whispered Louis.
Alphonse tried to bark, but it sounded like a burp.

"Hold on a minute," said the trainer. "What kind of dog is this?"

"He's a hairless spotted water spaniel from Scotland," explained Louis.

Alphonse quickly learned to SIT, STAY, and RETRIEVE.
He graduated at the top of his class.

"My parents will be very pleased," said Louis.

STOP AND THINK

Author's Craft Does the author's description of Alphonse seem funny? Why or why not?

But Louis's parents were not pleased when Alphonse
outgrew the sink and had to be moved to the bathtub.

"This shower is too crowded," complained Louis's father.

"This bathroom is a mess," moaned Louis's mother.

At least Louis's classmates enjoyed Alphonse, who was still making weekly visits.

"Wow! Show-and-tell is more fun than recess!" they yelled.

But one day Ms. Shelbert decided that Alphonse was not turning into an ordinary frog. She asked Louis to stop bringing him to school.

By the time summer vacation arrived, Alphonse had
outgrown the bathtub.

"We could buy the parking lot next door and build him
a swimming pool," suggested Louis.

"Be sensible," declared Louis's parents. "Swimming
pools are expensive. We're sorry, Louis, but this situation
has become impossible. Tomorrow you will have to take
your tadpole to the zoo."

"But I can't put my friend in a cage!" cried Louis.

That night Louis was very sad—until he remembered that the gym in the nearby high school had a swimming pool.

Louis hid Alphonse under a carpet and smuggled him inside.

"Nobody uses this place during the summer," whispered Louis. "You'll be safe here."

After making sure that Alphonse felt at home, Louis said good-bye. "I'll be back tomorrow with a big pile of cheeseburgers," he promised.

Louis came every afternoon to play with Alphonse.
In the mornings he earned the money for the
cheeseburgers by delivering newspapers.

The training continued as well.

Louis would say, "Alphonse, RETRIEVE!"

And Alphonse would succeed every time.

As summer vacation passed, Louis became more
and more worried about what would happen to
Alphonse when the high school kids returned.

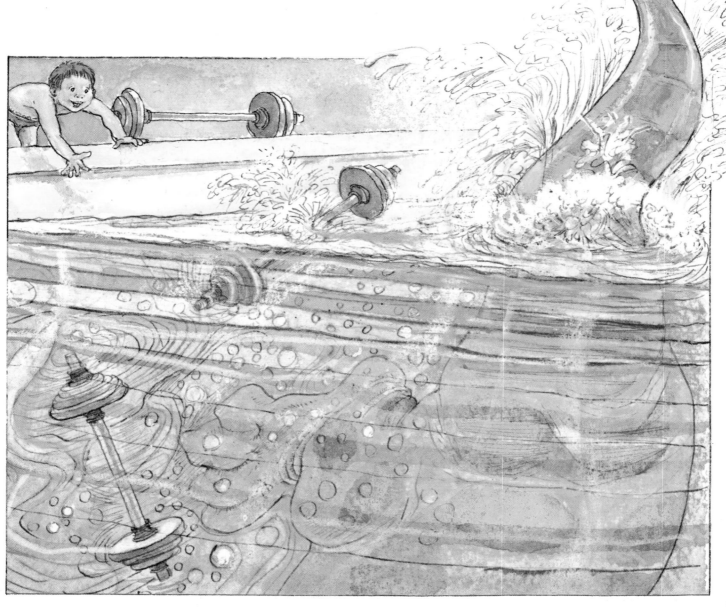

After his first day of classes Louis ran to the high
school, and found the gym bustling with activity. The
swim team was heading for the pool.

"STOP!" cried Louis.

"On your mark!" bellowed the coach. "Get set!"

"Excuse me, sir," said Louis.

"GO!" roared the coach.

Alphonse rose to the surface to welcome the swimmers.

"It's a submarine from another planet!" shrieked the coach.

"Call the police! Call the Navy!"

"No, it's only a tadpole," said Louis. "He's my pet."

The coach was upset and confused.

"You have until tomorrow," he cried, "to get that creature out of the pool!"

Louis telephoned his friend Ms. Seevers, the librarian, and asked for her help.

"I'll be right there!" she said.

Ms. Seevers rushed to meet Louis at the high school. When she saw Alphonse, she was so startled that she dropped her purse into the water.

"RETRIEVE!" said Louis. And Alphonse did.

"Where did this astounding animal come from?" cried Ms. Seevers.

"He was a birthday gift from my uncle," Louis replied.

Ms. Seevers telephoned Uncle McAllister.

"Oh, the wee tadpole?" he said. "Why, he came from the lake nearby. It's the one folks call Loch Ness."

"Brace yourself, Louis!" Ms. Seevers said. "I believe your uncle found the Loch Ness monster!"

"I don't care!" cried Louis. "Alphonse is my friend and I love him." He pleaded with Ms. Seevers to help him raise enough money to buy the parking lot so he could build a big swimming pool for Alphonse.

Suddenly Ms. Seevers had an idea. "Long ago a pirate ship sank in the harbor," she said. "No one has ever been able to find it—or its treasure chest. But perhaps we can!"

The next morning they drove to the harbor and rented a boat.

"This is a treasure chest," cried Louis. "RETRIEVE!"

Alphonse disappeared under the water and returned with the chest! It was filled with gold and jewels.

"Let's buy the parking lot and get to work!" cried Ms. Seevers.

Louis's parents were shocked to see a construction
crew in the parking lot.

"Louis!" they cried. "What in the world is going on here?"

"Alphonse found a pirate treasure ship," explained
Louis. "And we used part of our gold to buy you this present."

Louis's parents were shocked once again. "Tickets for a vacation cruise to Hawaii!" they gasped.

"And," said Louis, "you don't have to worry about us, because Granny has agreed to baby-sit." They hugged Louis. They kissed Alphonse.

"How soon can we leave?" they cried.

"Immediately," said Louis.

By the time Louis's parents returned, the swimming pool was being enjoyed by everyone in the city.

A week later Louis said, "Alphonse, tomorrow is my birthday, which means that you've been my best friend for a whole year."

The next day Uncle McAllister arrived for the party.

"Greetings, Louis my lad!" he exclaimed. "I've come with a curious stone from the hills of Scotland. Happy Birthday!"

"Wow! Thanks!" said Louis. Suddenly the stone began to tremble and crack . . .

STOP AND THINK

Infer/Predict Check your prediction about Alphonse. Was he a "perfect pet"?

370

Your Turn

A Tadpole's Life

Write Clues

In the beginning of *The Mysterious Tadpole,* the characters think that Alphonse is a tadpole. Think about how tadpoles grow into frogs. Then write clues from the story to prove that Alphonse is not a tadpole.

CONCLUSIONS

Where and When

The Mysterious Tadpole has more than one setting. Work with a partner to go back through the story. Discuss the settings. How do the story's words and pictures help you know each setting?

STORY STRUCTURE

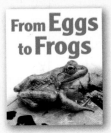
From Eggs to Frogs

From Egg to Tadpole

Many frogs start life as an egg that hatches in an ordinary pond. The young are called tadpoles. You may look at them suspiciously and feel confused. Why? Tadpoles look like tiny fish, not frogs.

Life Cycle of a Frog

A frog lays lots of eggs.

Tadpoles hatch from the eggs.

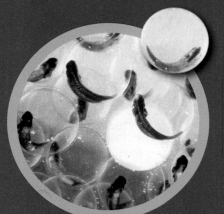

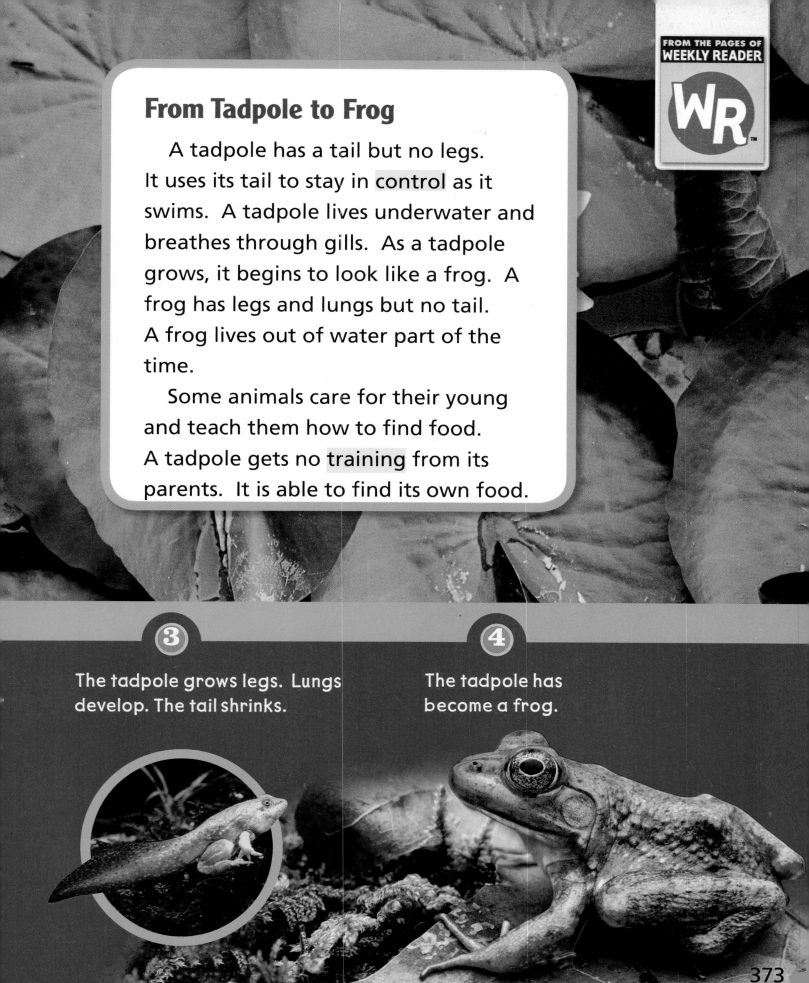

From Tadpole to Frog

A tadpole has a tail but no legs. It uses its tail to stay in control as it swims. A tadpole lives underwater and breathes through gills. As a tadpole grows, it begins to look like a frog. A frog has legs and lungs but no tail. A frog lives out of water part of the time.

Some animals care for their young and teach them how to find food. A tadpole gets no training from its parents. It is able to find its own food.

③ The tadpole grows legs. Lungs develop. The tail shrinks.

④ The tadpole has become a frog.

Frogs as Pets

It is a good idea to keep your frog in a fish tank, not a cage. Put water in the tank and rocks for the frog to climb on. Sensible owners handle their frogs gently so the frogs do not become upset. They give their frogs water, plants, and the good food they need.

Making Connections

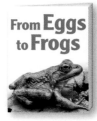

 Text to Self

Tell About a Gift How would you feel if you received Louis's birthday gift? Why?

 Text to Text

Compare Texts Steven Kellogg wrote *The Mysterious Tadpole*. Find another book by Steven Kellogg. Tell how the settings and events of the two stories are the same and different.

 Text to World

Connect to Science Think about real tadpoles and how they change into frogs. Choose another animal to research, such as caterpillars. Make a diagram to show how it changes as it grows.

Grammar

Contractions A **contraction** is a short way of writing two words. An **apostrophe** (') shows where letters were left out.

Academic Language

contraction
apostrophe

Whole Words	Contractions
do not	don't
that is	that's
is not	isn't
I am	I'm
I will	I'll
we are	we're
it is	it's

Try This! Read each sentence. Write the sentence using the correct contraction for the underlined words.

① I <u>do</u> <u>not</u> think that is a frog!

② <u>I</u> <u>am</u> sure <u>it</u> <u>is</u> a lake monster.

③ <u>We</u> <u>are</u> going to the library.

Conventions When you use contractions in your writing, be sure to spell them correctly. Remember to put the apostrophe (') in the right place.

Wrong	Correct
That is'nt a tadpole.	That isn't a tadpole.
Thats' a dinosaur!	That's a dinosaur!

Connect Grammar to Writing

When you edit your poem, make sure that contractions are spelled correctly and apostrophes are in the right place.

Write to Respond

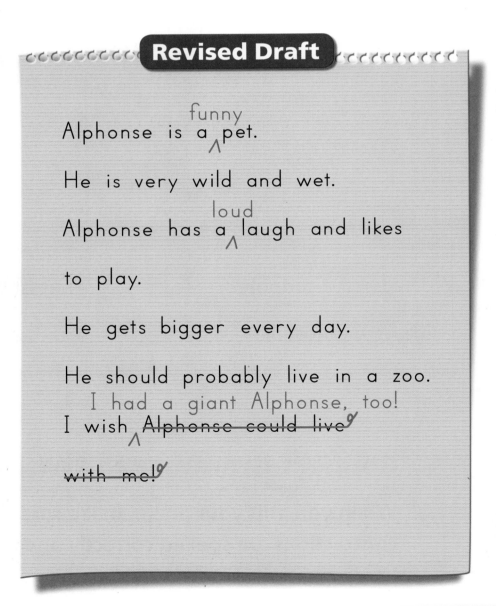

✔ **Word Choice** When you write a poem, use sensory words and details to make your feelings clear.

Luke drafted a poem in response to *The Mysterious Tadpole.* Later, he revised his writing to include more sensory words and details.

Writing Traits Checklist

✔ **Organization**
Did I write my poem with lines that rhyme?

✔ **Word Choice**
Did I use sense words and details?

✔ **Voice**
Did I use powerful language to show how I feel?

✔ **Sentence Fluency**
Do my sentences have a rhythm?

Revised Draft

Alphonse is a _{funny} pet.

He is very wild and wet.

Alphonse has a _{loud} laugh and likes

to play.

He gets bigger every day.

He should probably live in a zoo.
~~I wish Alphonse could live~~
I had a giant Alphonse, too!

~~with me!~~

A Funny Pet

by Luke Beem

Alphonse is a funny pet.

He is very wild and wet.

Alphonse has a loud laugh and likes to play.

He gets bigger every day.

He should probably live in a zoo.

I wish I had a giant Alphonse, too!

I added sensory words and details to make my poem more interesting.

Reading as a Writer

How do the sense words and details that Luke added make his poem more interesting? What words and details can you add to your own poem?

The Dog That Dug for Dinosaurs

La Brea Tar Pits

✔ TARGET VOCABULARY
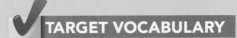

exact

discovered

remove

growled

amazed

explained

guard

souvenirs

Vocabulary
Reader

Context
Cards

Dinosaur Fossils

Vocabulary in Context

- **Study each Context Card.**

- **Make up a new sentence that uses a Vocabulary word.**

1

exact

The map showed the exact place to dig for old bones.

2

discovered

This old shark's tooth was discovered on a beach. It was found by a scientist.

3 **remove**

This scientist uses a brush to gently remove, or take away, sand.

4 **growled**

The dog growled and barked as it dug up the old bone.

5 **amazed**

The girl was amazed at the size of the dinosaur teeth in the museum.

6 **explained**

The man explained, or told, about the dinosaur.

7 **guard**

A guard makes sure no one touches anything in the museum.

8 **souvenirs**

He bought souvenirs to remember his day at the museum.

Background

Fossil Hunting Scientists have discovered fossils in many places. They collect fossils, they note its exact location. The fossil may then be placed in a museum under the watchful eyes of a guard. Museum visitors are amazed when they see a bone, tooth, or footprint of an animal that walked the earth millions of years ago!

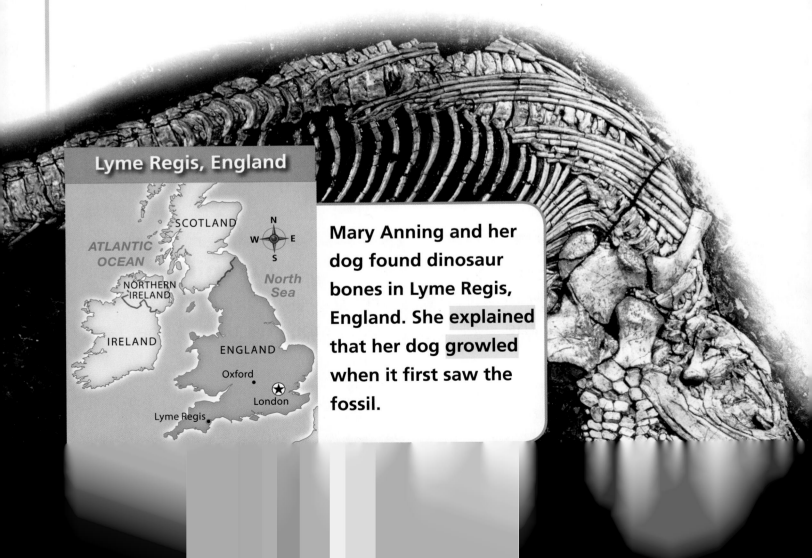

Lyme Regis, England

SCOTLAND

ATLANTIC OCEAN

NORTHERN IRELAND

North Sea

IRELAND

ENGLAND

Oxford

London

Lyme Regis

N W E S

Mary Anning and her dog found dinosaur bones in Lyme Regis, England. She explained that her dog growled when it first saw the fossil.

Comprehension

✔ **TARGET SKILL** **Fact and Opinion**

A fact is something that can be proved to be true or
false. An opinion is what someone believes or feels.
In *The Dog That Dug for Dinosaurs*, you will read facts
about what Mary and her dog find. You'll also read
people's opinions about them. Keep track of facts and
opinions in a chart like this one.

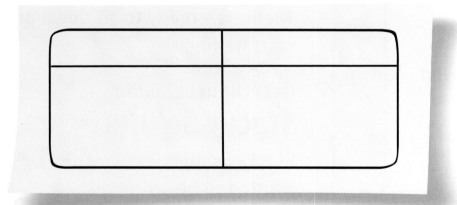

✔ **TARGET STRATEGY** **Question**

Ask yourself questions before, during, and after you
read *The Dog That Dug for Dinosaurs*. Use the answers
to find out if the author is stating a fact or an opinion.

Main Selection

✓ TARGET VOCABULARY

exact	amazed
discovered	explained
remove	guard
growled	souvenirs

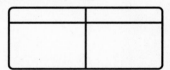

✓ TARGET SKILL

Fact and Opinion Tell if an idea can be proved or is a feeling.

✓ TARGET STRATEGY

Question Ask questions about what you are reading.

GENRE

A **biography** tells about events in a person's life.

MEET THE AUTHOR

Shirley Raye Redmond

At her home in New Mexico, Shirley Raye Redmond begins her day by waking up early and watching the many birds that come to the feeders in her yard. Then she's ready to sit down and start writing.

MEET THE ILLUSTRATOR

Stacey Schuett

Stacey Schuett wanted to be an artist or a writer ever since she was a kid. "I was a dreamy kind of little kid who loved to make stuff up," she says. She has illustrated many books, including ones on pirates and trees.

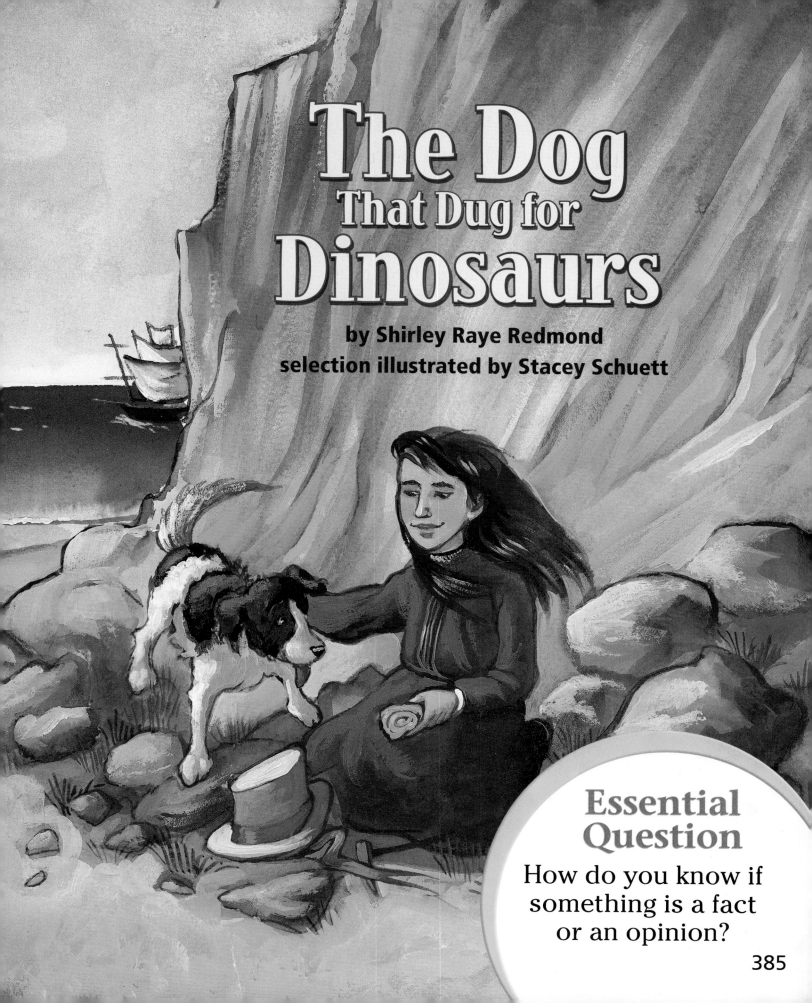

The Dog
That Dug for
Dinosaurs

by Shirley Raye Redmond
selection illustrated by Stacey Schuett

Essential Question

How do you know if something is a fact or an opinion?

A LONG, LONG TIME AGO, there
was a little dog named Tray. He was black-
and-white all over. He had friendly brown
eyes and a very wiggly tail. Tray lived in
England. Tray was a real dog, and this is
an honestly true story about him.

Tray loved two things most in the
whole world. First, he loved Mary Anning.
She was twelve years old and lived with her
family in a small cottage near the beach
in Lyme Regis. Secondly, Tray loved going
with Mary to dig for fossils.

So, what are fossils anyway? They are the remains of animals and plants that died a long time ago. When a leaf or bone gets pressed between layers of sea mud, it leaves an imprint. After many, many years, the mud hardens to rock.

Tray and Mary knew that they would find the very best fossils high up on the cliffs around the beach. They climbed up there every day.

Tray sniffed the rocks. *Sniff, sniff.* He pawed the dirt. *Scratch, scratch.* Mary used a small hammer and chisel. *Tap, tap, tap.*

With these tools, Mary carefully cut fossils out of the cliff, just as her father had shown her. Tray watched as she placed the fossils in her basket. Most of them looked like seashells. Mary and Tray sold them as souvenirs to the tourists that came by stagecoach to swim at the beach near their home.

One day Tray and Mary discovered some very large bones sticking out of the rocks. They were *huge*!

Tray growled and tried to dig the bones out.

Mary used her hands to brush away the loose dirt.

"Tray, we've discovered a monster!" she declared.

The bones were much too big for Tray and Mary to remove by themselves.

"I'll go for help," Mary said. "You stay here, Tray."

Tray barked loudly and sat down in front of the bones. He was a very good guard dog.

> **STOP AND THINK**
> **Question** What questions about fossils do these pages answer? What new questions about fossils do you have?

Mary ran all the way back to town and asked some grown-ups to help her. "Tray and I have found something really special in the cliff," she told them. "Just wait and see!"

When the men saw the giant rib bones in the side of the cliff, they were amazed. "What a beast!" they cried.

"Look at those sharp teeth!"

"Is it a crocodile?" one man asked. "Or a stubby whale?"

"We don't know what it is," Mary admitted. "But we know it's something special, don't we, Tray?"

Tray yipped and wagged his tail.

A rich man who lived nearby heard about the

sea monster. He hurried to see it for himself.

"I'll buy it!" he cried. "I will give it to the British Museum in London."

"Do you know what it is?" Mary asked.

"It is called an ichthyosaur (ICK-thee-uh-soar)," the man told her.

"That means 'fish lizard,'" he explained. "It's like a dinosaur with fins."

391

The amazing news spread about the gigantic fish lizard and the dog and little girl who had found it.

Soon many strangers came to Lyme Regis where Mary and Tray lived. They all wanted to hunt for fossils too. The men wore tall top hats. The women wore frilly bonnets. They carried pretty umbrellas called parasols.

Mary shook her head and smiled. She rubbed Tray's soft ears. They watched the strangers together.

"They don't have the right tools," Mary whispered. "They are wearing the wrong kinds of shoes. Aren't they silly, Tray?"

Tray yipped and chased his tail.

STOP AND THINK

Author's Craft How does the author help you understand how the strangers will have trouble finding fossils?

392

Curious scientists visited Lyme Regis too. One man came from the university in Oxford. His name was William Buckland. He went to the old carpenter's shop where Mary and Tray sold their fossils.

"Can you show me where you found your ichthyosaur, young lady?" he asked politely. "Do you think you could find the exact spot again?"

"Tray can find it," Mary boasted.

Together Mary and Mr. Buckland followed the little dog across the beach and up to the cliffs.

Tray sniffed the rocks. *Sniff, sniff.*

He pawed the dirt. *Scratch, scratch.*

Suddenly he yipped. Then he sat down. Mary pointed. It was the exact place where she had discovered the strange fish lizard!

"What an intelligent dog!" Mr. Buckland declared.

Tray wagged his tail.

Tray and Mary continued to dig for fossils. They were very careful. Mary watched for falling rocks, like her dad told her. Tray looked out for storms and high tides. Then one day they discovered another giant creature.

"Look, Tray!" Mary cried. "Is it a sea dragon?"

Tray sniffed the skeleton and snapped
at it with his teeth. The creature had a long, long neck.
Its backbone was like a humped turtle shell. Instead of
feet and legs, it had four large paddles.

But it wasn't a sea dragon.

Mr. Buckland called it a plesiosaur
(PLEE-zee-uh-soar).

One day, Tray and Mary found a fossil that no one in England had ever found before. This one had huge bony wings like a bat and a long sharp jaw.

Tray growled.

"It looks like a gigantic flying lizard!" Mary declared.

The scientists thought so too, and that's why they named it a pterodactyl (TAIR-uh-DACK-til).

That means "lizard with wings."

Over the years, Tray, Mary, and Mr. Buckland became good friends.

They showed him where to find the best fossils in Lyme Regis.

 STOP AND THINK
Fact and Opinion What fact do you learn about Mary's find? What is her opinion about it?

Mr. Buckland brought books about dinosaurs for Mary. He brought beef bones for Tray. Mary, with Tray on her lap, studied her books every day.

When Tray's whiskers turned gray and Mary was all grown up, they still collected fossils and sold them in the old carpenter's shop. There were boxes and baskets filled with fossils on the floor and on the shelves. Some of the fossil creatures were so big they couldn't fit through the door!

Sometimes children and tourists stopped in to buy fossils of ancient sand dollars or tiny fish and curly shells. Many scientists came to the shop to buy fossils too. They brought carts and wagons to haul away the really large ones.

Tray and Mary Anning became very famous. Today, if you go to the Natural History Museum in London, you can see the large fossils they discovered together.

You can also see a famous painting of Mary holding her fossil basket, and Tray, the dog that dug for dinosaurs.

Your Turn

Dino Discovery

Make a Model

Work with a partner. Imagine that you and your partner have discovered a new dinosaur. What will you name it? What does it look like? Make a model of your new dinosaur. Use clay or art scraps. Then share your model with the class. PARTNERS

Turn and Talk — ## Fact or Opinion?

With a partner, look back at page 392 of the selection. Which sentences on the page include facts? Which include opinions? Discuss how you know. FACT AND OPINION

✓ **TARGET VOCABULARY**

exact	amazed
discovered	explained
remove	guard
growled	souvenirs

GENRE

Informational text gives facts about a topic. This is a newspaper article.

TEXT FOCUS

A **time line** is a line that shows the order in which events happened.

DAILY NEWS

FRIDAY, JANUARY 18

La Brea Tar Pits

by Ciara McLaughlin

Did you know that Los Angeles, California, is famous for its tar pits? They are the La Brea Tar Pits, to be exact. Scientists remove lots of fossils from them. Many people are amazed to see the fossils.

La Brea is one of the best places in the world to find fossils.

Life-size statues of mammoths at the La Brea Tar Pits

Scientists have explained that Los Angeles was once cooler and wetter than it is today. They know this because fossils of plants and animals that lived only in cool wet places have been discovered there. These plants and animals lived a very long time ago. The animals included big cats with huge teeth. Imagine how they growled! Other animals had to be on guard if they did not want to be eaten.

A saber-toothed cat skull

At times, wolves chased mammoths into tar pits. Then the sticky tar trapped them all. The trapped animals died. Over time, they became fossils.

The tar still traps living things. In time, they may become fossils. People may find them and keep them as souvenirs.

Scientists searching for fossils at the La Brea Tar Pits

La Brea Time Line

More than 100,000 years ago	About 100,000 years ago	About 40,000 years ago	Today
Area covered by water	Water goes down, and land appears	First plants and animals trapped	Surrounded by a busy city

Making Connections

La Brea
Tar Pits

 Text to Self

Tell About a Discovery How does finding dinosaur bones change Mary's life? How would it change your life?

 Text to Text

Choosing Resources Think about *The Dog That Dug for Dinosaurs* and "La Brea Tar Pits." Which would be more helpful if you wanted to write a report about dinosaurs? Explain.

 Text to World

Connect to Social Studies Why is Mary Anning an important person? Write about how her discoveries might have helped people. Then work with a partner to revise your writing so it is clearer.

Grammar

What Is an Adverb? An **adverb** is a word that describes a **verb**. An adverb can tell how something happens. It can also tell when something happens.

Academic Language

adverb

verb

Adverbs That Tell How	Adverbs That Tell When
Tray and I slowly dug in the dirt.	Before the trip, I got some tools.
We pulled out the fossil gently.	Next, I put on some gloves.

Turn and Talk **Work with a partner. Choose an adverb from the box to complete each sentence. Then read the sentence aloud.**

loudly	after	sometimes

❶ _____ lunch, I sold the fossil.

❷ My dog barked _____ to warn of danger.

❸ _____ we need more help.

Sentence Fluency Sometimes you may write two sentences with adverbs that tell about the same verb. Join the sentences, using **and** between the two adverbs. This will make your writing smoother.

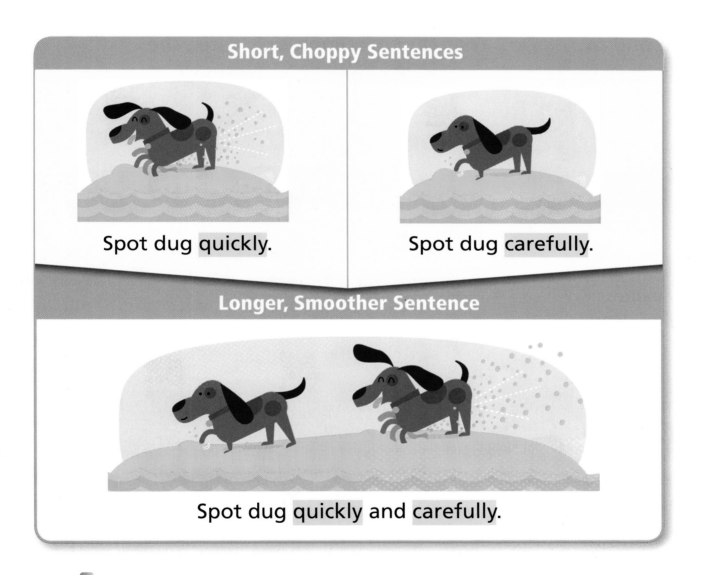

Short, Choppy Sentences

Spot dug quickly.

Spot dug carefully.

Longer, Smoother Sentence

Spot dug quickly and carefully.

Connect Grammar to Writing

When you revise your opinion paragraph, combine sentences with adverbs that tell about the same verbs.

Write to Respond

In an **opinion paragraph**, adjectives can help make your opinion clearer to your reader.

Gina wrote a draft of an opinion paragraph to respond to *The Dog That Dug for Dinosaurs*. Later, she added some adjectives to help express her opinion.

Writing Traits Checklist

☑ **Ideas**
Did I express my opinion clearly?

☑ **Voice**
Does my writing sound like me?

☑ **Word Choice**
Did I use adjectives to express my opinion?

☑ **Conventions**
Did I use resources to check my spelling?

Revised Draft

I think some of the people

who came to see the fossils

were silly. The silliest ones were
                                    fancy
all dressed up in their ∧ clothes.
                          appropriate
They weren't dressed in ∧ clothes

for hunting for fossils. They had

on dressy shoes and couldn't
                rocky
walk on the ∧ ground.

Some Were Silly

by Gina Greco

I think some of the people who came to see the fossils were silly. The silliest ones were all dressed up in their fancy clothes. They weren't dressed in appropriate clothes for hunting for fossils. They had on dressy shoes and couldn't walk on the rocky ground. Some of the other people don't seem silly to me. The curious scientists who came were really interested in Mary and Tray's unusual discoveries.

> I added adjectives to help express my opinion.

Reading as a Writer

How do the adjectives Gina added help show how she feels? What adjectives can you add to your response?

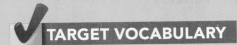
✓ **TARGET VOCABULARY**

astronomy

orbit

space

explored

repair

float

force

future

Vocabulary Reader   Context Cards

410

Vocabulary in Context

● Study each **Context Card**.

● Talk about a picture. Use a different Vocabulary word from the one on the card.

1   **astronomy**

Astronomy is the study of the planets, the stars, and other objects in space.

2   **orbit**

Earth is one of the planets that orbit, or go around, the Sun.

3 **space**

The area beyond Earth is sometimes called outer space.

4 **explored**

In 1969, the first people landed on the Moon and explored it.

5 **repair**

This astronaut is helping to repair, or fix, the space shuttle.

6 **float**

Astronauts can float from place to place. They are weightless in space!

7 **force**

Gases shoot out of a rocket with enough force to push it off Earth.

8 **future**

In the future, a long time from now, people might live in space.

Background

✓ **TARGET VOCABULARY** **Life in Space** In the future, people may live on space stations that orbit a planet. What will life be like in space? People might study astronomy or do a job such as helping to repair the space station. The lack of the force of gravity will make mealtime tricky. The food must be attached to trays. Otherwise, the meal will float away!

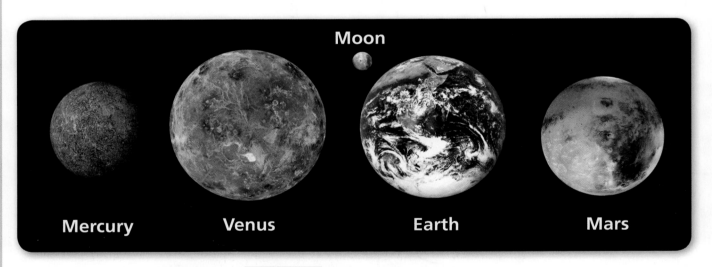

Moon

Mercury   Venus   Earth   Mars

People have already explored Earth and the Moon. Where do you think they might go next?

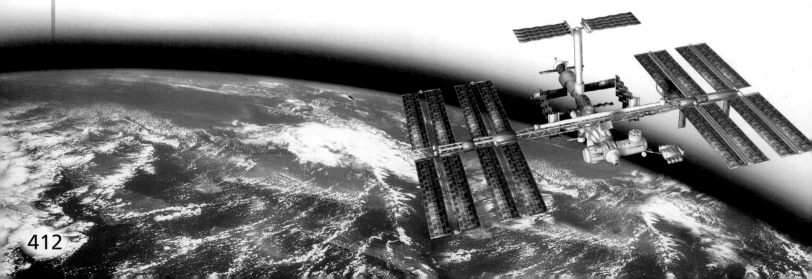

412

Comprehension

✔ **TARGET SKILL**   **Text and Graphic Features**

The headings, photos, and other features in *Working in Space* help you understand more about what astronauts do. As you read, use a chart like this to list some text and graphic features. Then tell why you think the author used each one.

Text or Graphic Feature	Page Number	Purpose

✔ **TARGET STRATEGY**   **Analyze/Evaluate**

As you read, pay attention to the ways text and graphic features help you understand the author's ideas. Then decide how well the author explained how living in space differs from living on Earth.

✓ **TARGET VOCABULARY**

astronomy	repair
orbit	float
space	force
explored	future

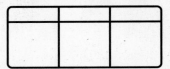

✓ **TARGET SKILL**
Text and Graphic Features Tell how words go with photos.

✓ **TARGET STRATEGY**
Analyze/Evaluate Tell how you feel about the text, and why.

GENRE
Informational text gives facts about a topic.

MEET THE AUTHOR
Patricia Whitehouse

Have you ever wondered what it would be like to explore space? Patricia Whitehouse has, but she's a writer, not an astronaut. In fact, she's written several books about space. She has also written a series of books about zoo animals, including *Sea Lion*, *Ostrich*, and *Alligator*.

Working in SPACE

by
Patricia
Whitehouse

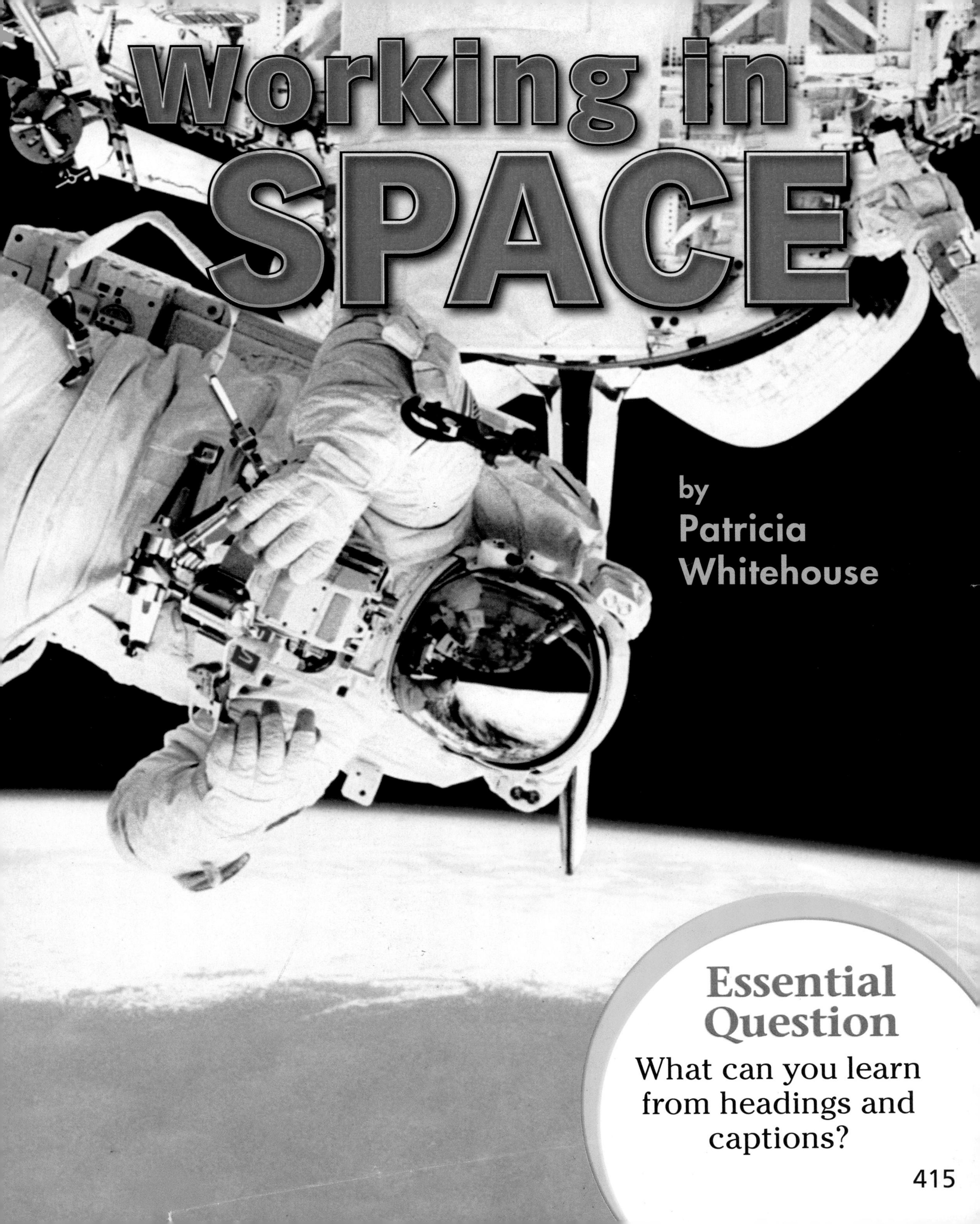

Essential Question

What can you learn from headings and captions?

pilot

commander

Leaving Earth

Five, four, three, two, one . . . The space shuttle blasts off! Astronauts on the shuttle are going to work. Some stay on the shuttle and some work at the space station.

Two astronauts have already started working. The shuttle commander is in charge of the shuttle and crew. The pilot flies the shuttle.

Jobs in Space

Three mission specialists are on board the shuttle. They work on experiments or climb outside to fix satellites. They have to prepare the food, too.

A company or university might want to do an experiment in space. An astronaut called a payload specialist will work on the experiment.

Working in Space

The space shuttle travels around Earth so fast that it is like falling. Everything inside falls, too. It makes astronauts and everything in the shuttle float around. This is called weightlessness.

Astronauts do not work at desks and tables. Everything would float off because of weightlessness! They have to use tape to stick everything down.

Astronaut Training

Astronauts need special training. They study at a university and then do a year of basic astronaut training. Astronauts learn math, science, and astronomy. They also practice using space equipment.

Astronauts practice working in water. Their suits are filled with air to make them float. It helps them learn what it will be like in space.

Under water it feels like you weigh less than on land. This is what it is like in space.

STOP AND THINK
Analyze/Evaluate How do you know that training is important to the astronauts?

This experiment measures how much air an astronaut uses while exercising.

Experiments on Astronauts

Living in space can change the human body. Astronauts often take part in experiments to find out how to keep healthy in space.

In space, astronauts do not use their bones and muscles very much. They can get very weak. Astronauts need to exercise every day in space.

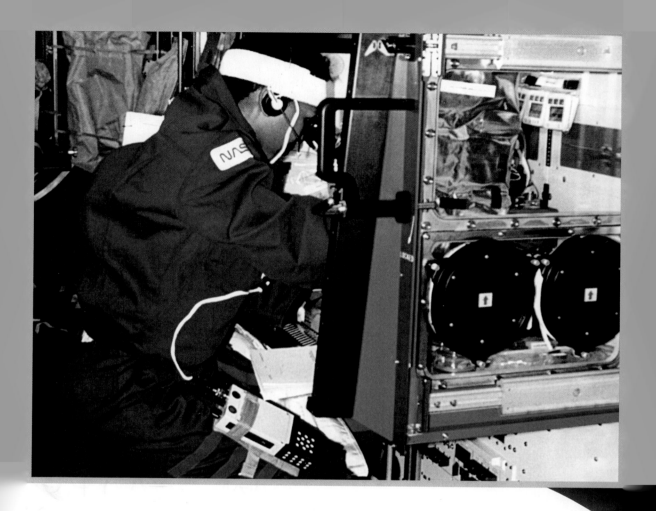

Other Experiments

Scientists want to find out how living in space affects plants and animals. Astronauts have taken bees, ants, and fish into space to see what happens to them.

Astronauts also test to see what happens to chemicals in space. They use a sealed box with gloves sticking into it so the experiment does not float away.

Taking Photos in Space

Astronauts also take pictures and videos of themselves living in space. The photos help people on Earth understand what it is like to live in space.

Astronauts take pictures of Earth, too. These photos are often beautiful as well as educational. They can show Earth's landforms and weather in ways that can never be seen from Earth.

erupting volcano

STOP AND THINK
Text and Graphic Features How do the heading and photos help you understand the text?

Fixing Satellites

Satellites that orbit Earth sometimes break down and need repair. They cannot be taken to a workshop. Specially trained astronauts have to fix them.

The shuttle pilot finds the satellite and moves the shuttle near it. An astronaut uses the shuttle's robotic arm to pull the satellite into the shuttle's cargo bay.

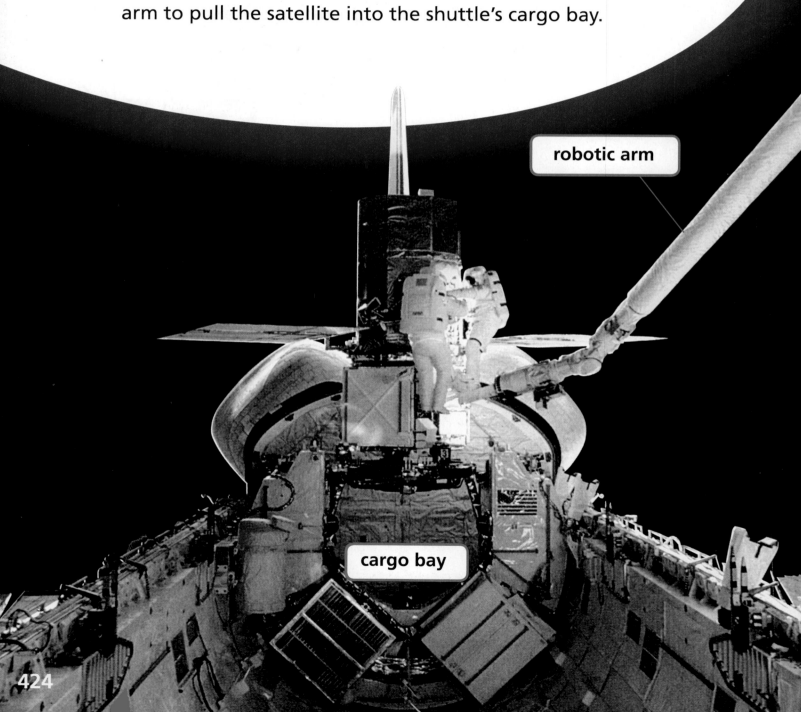

robotic arm

cargo bay

Spacesuits protect astronauts, give them air, and keep them cool.

Working Outside

People who work outside on Earth sometimes wear special clothing. Some clothing protects workers. Some clothing is brightly colored so the workers can be seen easily.

Astronauts wear special clothing when they work outside, too. Outside the shuttle there is no air to breathe, and it can be uncomfortably warm.

Suiting Up

Astronauts must wear special spacesuits to go out of the shuttle. The spacesuits allow the astronauts to breathe and stay cool. Every part of their bodies is covered.

Astronauts use an airlock to leave the shuttle. The airlock is a room between the shuttle and space. In the airlock, the door to the shuttle seals shut, and then the outer door into space can be opened.

STOP AND THINK
Author's Craft Why do you think the author has chosen to describe an airlock?

Spacesuits are sealed at the neck, wrists, and waist.

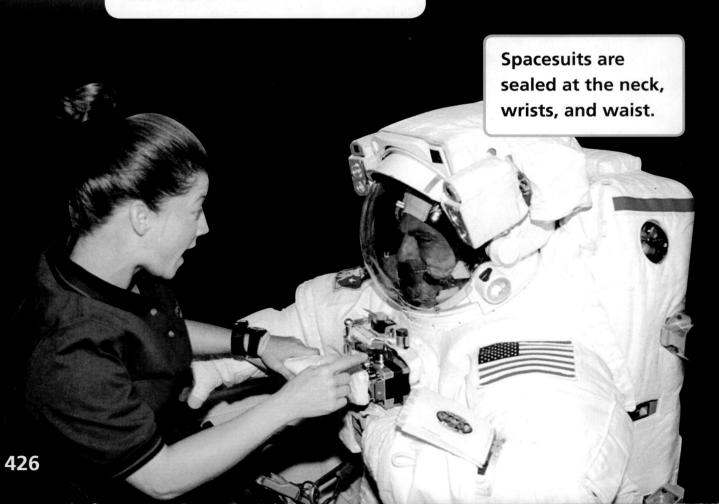

Gloves and Ties

Spacesuits are hard to move in. Gloves make finger movements tricky. Jobs that take a few minutes on Earth can take hours in space.

In space, astronauts and equipment can float away. Astronauts tie equipment to their suits. Sometimes astronauts are tied to the shuttle, too.

Moving Around

Sometimes astronauts need to move around a lot outside the shuttle. They wear a backpack with rocket power called a Manned Maneuvering Unit, or MMU.

The MMU tank is filled with gas. The astronaut squeezes a handle, and gas comes out with enough force to move the astronaut around.

Working on Other Worlds

Twelve astronauts have worked on the Moon. They collected rocks from the Moon's surface. This helped scientists learn about Earth and about living on other worlds.

Scientists explored Mars using a remote-controlled robot called Sojourner. Scientists think that in the future people might be able to live and work on Mars.

Sojourner

Fun Jobs

Guessing Game

Which space job sounds like fun to you? Choose one of the jobs that you read about in *Working in Space.* Act it out for a small group to guess. Give word clues if needed. SMALL GROUPS

Turn and Talk — Helpful Captions

Look back at page 419. Read the words and look at the picture. Then work with a partner to write a caption on a sticky note for the photograph. Talk about how your caption tells about the picture. TEXT AND GRAPHIC FEATURES

This astronaut is

Space Poems

As you read these space poems, listen for words that rhyme.

De Koven

You are a dancy little thing,
You are a rascal, star!
You seem to be so near to me,
And yet you are so far.

If I could get you in my hands
You'd never get away.
I'd keep you with me always.
You'd shine both night and day.

by Gwendolyn Brooks

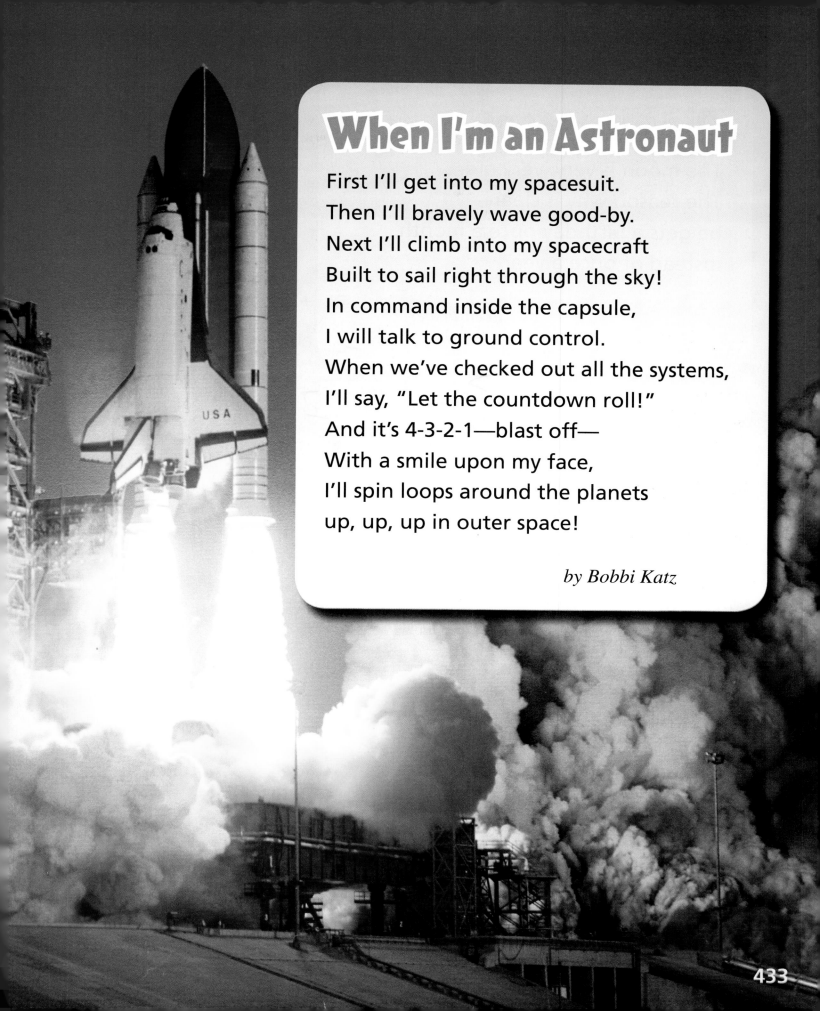

When I'm an Astronaut

First I'll get into my spacesuit.
Then I'll bravely wave good-by.
Next I'll climb into my spacecraft
Built to sail right through the sky!
In command inside the capsule,
I will talk to ground control.
When we've checked out all the systems,
I'll say, "Let the countdown roll!"
And it's 4-3-2-1—blast off—
With a smile upon my face,
I'll spin loops around the planets
up, up, up in outer space!

by Bobbi Katz

Old Man Moon

The moon is very, very old.
The reason why is clear—
he gets a birthday once a month,
instead of once a year.

by Aileen Fisher

Write a Space Poem

Discuss how the poems you read use rhyme, repetition, and rhythm. Then write a poem about astronomy or what you would do if you explored space in the future. Use float, repair, force, and orbit in the poem.

Making Connections

Text to Self

Respond to Facts Which facts in *Working in Space* do you find most surprising? Explain your ideas to a partner.

Text to Text

Connect to Social Studies How are the astronauts in *Working in Space* and the scientists in *The Dog That Dug for Dinosaurs* (Lesson 27) alike and different? Make and present a poster that compares their jobs.

Both Mary Anning and astronauts use special tools for their jobs.

Text to World

Research Jobs Astronauts use a lot of science and math in their jobs. Research other jobs that involve science or math. Work with your class to list them.

Grammar

Possessive Nouns A **possessive noun** shows that a person or animal owns or has something. Add an **apostrophe** (') and *-s* to a singular noun to make it a possessive noun. Add just an apostrophe to a noun that ends in *-s* to make it a possessive noun.

Academic Language

possessive noun

apostrophe

Singular Possessive Nouns	Plural Possessive Nouns
one astronaut's glove	many astronauts' gloves
a pilot's training	two pilots' training
a crew's job	five crews' jobs

Try This! **Write each possessive noun correctly by adding an apostrophe (') or an apostrophe and *-s* to the name of the owner.**

1. Jeff trip

2. two students experiments

3. an astronaut view

436

Sentence Fluency Use possessive nouns in your writing. They can help you avoid wordy sentences.

Wordy Sentence	Sentence with Possessive Noun
The suit belonging to the astronaut is made for space travel.	The astronaut's suit is made for space travel.

Connect Grammar to Writing

When you revise your response paragraph, look for places where you can use a possessive noun to fix a wordy sentence.

Write to Respond

When you write a **response paragraph**, use only details that support your opinions.

Arianna drafted a response paragraph about *Working in Space*. Later, she revised her draft by taking out details that didn't belong.

Writing Traits Checklist

☑ Ideas
Do all the details support my opinion?

☑ Organization
Did I begin by stating my opinion?

☑ Sentence Fluency
Did I combine sentences that have the same naming part?

☑ Conventions
Did I punctuate my sentences correctly?

Revised Draft

I would love to be an astronaut! I like adventure. ~~My family goes on a trip every summer.~~ Science is my favorite subject, and I know all about space and the solar system. ~~Mercury is the planet closest to the sun.~~ In Science period, I've read about what astronauts do.

I Want to Be an Astronaut

by Arianna Gerard

I would love to be an astronaut! I like adventure. Science is my favorite subject, and I know all about space and the solar system. In Science period, I've read about what astronauts do. They get training in certain fields. I would like to learn how to repair space stations. I could float in space and make sure the spaceship is OK. I think that would be very exciting!

> I took out details that didn't connect to my opinion.

Reading as a Writer

Which details did Arianna take out? Which details should you take out of your paragraph?

439

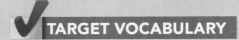
TARGET VOCABULARY

search

contained

startled

odd

leaned

tossed

grateful

village

Vocabulary   Context
Reader   Cards

Vocabulary in Context

- Study each **Context Card**.

- Place the Vocabulary words in alphabetical order.

1
search
It is fun to search for buried treasure. You never know what you will find!

2
contained
This old box contained jewels, coins, and other treasures.

3 startled

The divers were startled to find treasure at the bottom of the ocean.

4 odd

Do you think it is odd, or strange, to look for buried treasure?

5 leaned

The woman leaned over to get a better view of the whale near the ship.

6 tossed

They tossed the supplies into the trunk to pack for their vacation.

7 grateful

The museum was very grateful, or thankful, to get the old statues.

8 village

This village is near the ocean. People find coins buried on the beach.

Background

✔ **TARGET VOCABULARY** **Wishes** Have you ever leaned over a village wishing well and dropped in a coin? Would you search for a four-leaf clover to wish upon? People are usually grateful if a wish comes true. Wishes can come true in odd ways. King Midas's wish contained something bad. He wished everything he touched would turn to gold. He was startled when everything did turn to gold, including his daughter.

This girl has tossed a penny over her shoulder into a wishing well. What do you think she wished for?

Comprehension

✔ **TARGET SKILL** **Understanding Characters**

Two of Everything tells how the Haktaks' lucky find causes a big problem. As you read, pay attention to what the characters say, do, and think. These details are clues that tell what they are like. You can write important details in a chart like this one.

Words	Actions	Thoughts

✔ **TARGET STRATEGY** **Summarize**

Knowing what Mr. and Mrs. Haktak are like will help you understand how they are able to solve their problem. Use the details in your chart to summarize their actions and to tell what they are like.

Main Selection

✓ TARGET VOCABULARY

search	leaned
contained	tossed
startled	grateful
odd	village

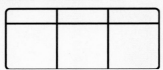

✓ TARGET SKILL

Understanding Characters Tell more about characters.

✓ TARGET STRATEGY

Summarize Stop to tell important events as you read.

GENRE

A **folktale** is a story that is often told by people of a country. Use the genre to set a purpose for reading.

MEET THE AUTHOR AND ILLUSTRATOR

Lily Toy Hong

Lily Toy Hong enjoys camping, getting together with her large family, and eating Chinese food. She also loves learning about her parents' native country, China, and its many legends and folktales. "One day I would love to visit China and explore the land of my forefathers," she says, "and maybe discover more folktales."

Two of Everything

by Lily Toy Hong

Essential Question

What clues help you understand a story character?

445

Once long ago, in a humble little hut, lived Mr. Haktak and his wife, Mrs. Haktak. They were old and very poor. What little they ate came from their tiny garden.

In a lucky year when the harvest was plentiful, Mr. Haktak had a little extra to take to the village. There he traded turnips, potatoes, and other vegetables for clothing, lamp oil, and fresh seeds.

One spring morning when Mr. Haktak was digging in his garden, his shovel struck something hard. Puzzled, he dug deeper into the dark ground until he came upon an ancient pot made of brass.

"How odd," said Mr. Haktak to himself. "To think that I have been digging here all these years and never came upon this pot before! I will take it home. Maybe Mrs. Haktak can find some use for it."

STOP AND THINK

Author's Craft What story details do you learn from the person telling the story? Which details do you learn from what Mr. Haktak says?

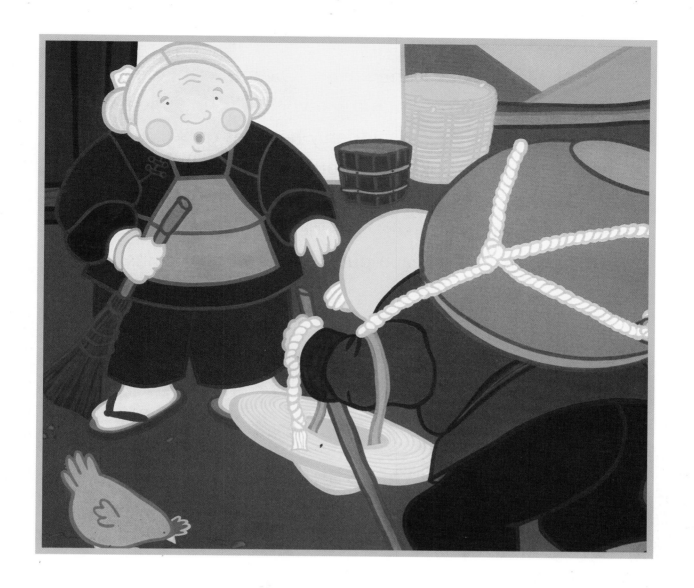

The pot was big and heavy for old Mr. Haktak.
As he stumbled along, his purse, which contained his
last five gold coins, fell to the ground. He tossed it
into the pot for safekeeping and staggered home.

His wife greeted him at the door. "Dear husband,
what a strange pot!" Mr. Haktak explained how he
found the pot. "I wonder what we can do with it,"
said Mrs. Haktak. "It looks too large to cook in and
too small to bathe in."

As Mrs. Haktak leaned over to peer into the pot, her hairpin—the only one she owned—fell in. She felt around in the pot, and suddenly her eyes grew round with surprise. "Look!" she shouted. "I've pulled out TWO hairpins, exactly alike, and TWO purses, too!" Sure enough, the purses were identical, and so were the hairpins. Inside each purse were five gold coins!

Mr. Haktak was so excited he jumped up and down. "Let's put my winter coat inside the pot. If we are lucky again the pot will make two coats, and then we will both stay warm." So into the pot went one coat—and out came TWO coats.

They began to search the house and quickly put more things into the magical pot. "If only we had some meat," wished Mr. Haktak, "or fresh fruit, or one delicious sweet cake."

Mrs. Haktak smiled. "I know how we can get anything we want," she said. She put their ten coins into one purse, then threw it into the pot. She pulled out two purses with ten coins in each.

"What a clever wife I have!" cried Mr. Haktak. "Each time we do this we will have twice as much money as before!"

The Haktaks worked late into the night, filling and emptying the pot until the floor was covered with coins.

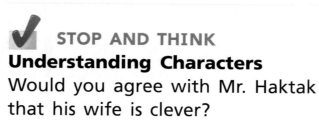

STOP AND THINK
Understanding Characters
Would you agree with Mr. Haktak that his wife is clever?

Morning came, and off went Mr. Haktak with a long list of things to buy in the village. Instead of vegetables, his basket was full of gold coins.

Mrs. Haktak finished all of her chores and sat down to enjoy a cup of tea. She sipped her tea and admired the brass pot. Then with a grateful heart, she knelt and embraced it. "Dear pot, I do not know where you came from, but you are my best friend." She stooped over the pot to look inside.

At that very moment, Mr. Haktak returned. His arms were so full of packages that he had to kick the door open. Bang! Mrs. Haktak was so startled that she lost her balance and fell headfirst into the pot!

Mr. Haktak ran over and grabbed his wife's legs. He pulled and tugged until she slid out onto the floor. But when he looked at the pot again, he gasped. Two more legs were sticking straight out of it! Naturally, he took hold of the ankles and pulled.

Out came a second person! She looked exactly like his wife.

The new Mrs. Haktak sat silently on the floor looking lost. But the first Mrs. Haktak cried, "I am your one and only wife! Put that woman back into the pot right now!"

Mr. Haktak yelled, "No! If I put her back we will not have two women but THREE. One wife is enough for me!"

He backed away from his angry wife, and tripped and fell headfirst into the pot himself!

Both Mrs. Haktaks rushed to rescue him. Each grasped an ankle, and together they pulled him out. There were two more legs in the pot. So they pulled out the other Mr. Haktak, too.

"Just what use does one Mr. Haktak have for another!" Mr. Haktak cried angrily. "This pot is not as wonderful as we thought it to be. Now even our troubles are beginning to double."

But his wife had been thinking while he was yelling.

STOP AND THINK
Summarize Summarize how two Mrs. Haktaks and two Mr. Haktaks come to be.

457

"Calm down," she said. "It is good that the other Mrs. Haktak has her own Mr. Haktak. Perhaps we will become best of friends. After all, we are so alike he will be a brother to you and she a sister to me. With our pot we can make two of everything, so there will be plenty to go around."

And that is what they did. The Haktaks built two fine new homes. Each house had identical teapots, rice bowls, silk embroideries, and bamboo furniture.

From the outside, the houses looked exactly alike, but there was one difference. Hidden in one house was a big brass pot. Of course, the Haktaks were always very careful not to fall into it again!

The new Haktaks and the old Haktaks did become good friends. The neighbors thought that the Haktaks had grown so rich that they decided to have two of everything—even themselves!

A Clever Wife

Write a Response

On page 452, Mr. Haktak says that his wife is very clever. Do you agree that Mrs. Haktak is clever? Write a paragraph to explain your opinion using details from the story.

RESPONSE TO LITERATURE

Turn and Talk — My Favorite Thing

With a partner, look back through *Two of Everything*. Think about the things that the Haktaks put in the pot on purpose. Discuss with your partner what you think the characters might want to put in the pot next and why.

UNDERSTANDING CHARACTERS

✔ TARGET VOCABULARY

search	leaned
contained	tossed
startled	grateful
odd	village

GENRE

Traditional tales are stories that have been told for many years.

TEXT FOCUS

A **folktale** is a story passed down to explain or entertain.

Readers' Theater

Stone Soup

adapted by
Greta McLaughlin

Cast of Characters

Narrator	Traveler	Boy

Narrator: A hungry man set out to search for food. He stopped in a village and knocked on the door of every home.

Traveler: Please, could you share some food with me?

Narrator: It startled the villagers to see a stranger. They would not share with him.

Narrator: The man leaned against a well. He took a pot out of his sack and filled it with water.

Boy: What are you doing?

Traveler: I've tossed a stone into my pot so I can make stone soup.

Boy: That's odd. Is stone soup good?

Traveler: It is. But the soup would be better if I had a carrot.

Boy: Grandma grows carrots. I'll ask her for one.

Traveler: Thank you. Please, ask her to join us for soup.

Narrator: The boy stopped at all the villagers' homes. He gathered food to put into the pot. Soon the soup contained carrots, green beans, potatoes, and more.

Boy: Is the soup ready?

Traveler: Yes, it is just right.

Narrator: The man shared his soup with the grateful villagers. In turn, they made sure that he never went hungry again.

Making Connections

Text to Self

Write a Paragraph What do the Haktaks do when they find the magical pot? Would you do the same thing? Write to explain.

Text to Text

Discuss Story Structures Think about the characters, settings, and plots of *Two of Everything* and *Stone Soup*. Work with a partner to compare the two stories.

Text to World

Connect to Traditional Tales What other traditional tales have you read? What features did they share with *Two of Everything*? Discuss your ideas with the class.

Grammar

Possessive Pronouns A **possessive pronoun** is a **pronoun** that shows ownership. The possessive pronouns *my* and *your* are used before nouns. The possessive pronouns *mine* and *yours* are used after nouns. *His* can be used before or after nouns.

Academic Language

possessive pronoun

pronoun

Pronouns Used Before Nouns	Pronouns Used Alone
My purse is new.	The new purse is mine.
Jess has your small pot.	The small pot is yours.
His house is the biggest.	The biggest house is his.

Turn and Talk **Work with a partner. Read each sentence aloud. Name the possessive pronouns.**

1. Carmen showed the pot to her class.

2. I couldn't believe my eyes.

3. Mark said the pot was his.

4. I wanted the pot to be mine!

Sentence Fluency You can use possessive pronouns in place of repeated possessive nouns. This can make your writing better.

Repeated Possessive Noun	Possessive Pronoun
Sal said that the twins were brothers of Sal's.	Sal said that the twins were brothers of hers.

Connect Grammar to Writing

As you revise your response essay next week, look for possessive nouns that you can change to possessive pronouns. This will make your writing smoother.

Write to Respond

✅**Ideas**   When you write a **response to literature** include reasons for your opinion. Give examples to support each of your reasons.

Cooper planned his essay in response to *Two of Everything*. He thought of reasons for his opinion. Then he used an opinion chart to add examples.

Writing Process Checklist

▶ **Prewrite**

☑ **Did I identify my opinion about this story?**

☑ **Did I give reasons for my opinion?**

☑ **Did I come up with good examples for each of my reasons?**

Draft

Revise

Edit

Publish and Share

Exploring a Topic

The pot was good for the Haktaks. Why?

Reason 1:	Reason 2:
The pot doubled everything for them.	They ended up happy after all.

Opinion Chart

My Opinion: The pot was good for the Haktaks.

Reason 1: The pot doubled everything for them.	Reason 2: They ended up happy after all.
Example 1: Mr. Haktak put his coins in the pot, and it doubled his money.	Example 1: The pot gave them a second home and everything to put in it.
Example 2: The pot gave them a second Mr. and Mrs. Haktak.	Example 2: They made friends with the new Mr. and Mrs. Haktak.

I gave reasons and examples to support my opinion.

Reading as a Writer

What examples did Cooper add to support his reasons? Which examples can you give to support your opinion?

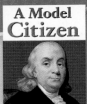

✔ **TARGET VOCABULARY**

inventions

remarkable

designed

amounts

accomplishments

achieve

composed

result

Vocabulary Reader	Context Cards

Vocabulary in Context

- Study each **Context Card**.

- Tell a story about two pictures, using the Vocabulary words.

1 inventions

Wheels are one of the inventions that we use in many different ways.

2 remarkable

The telephone is a remarkable invention that lets you talk to people.

3 designed

These boys designed and built a truck from blocks that snap together.

4 amounts

These light bulbs give off different amounts of light.

5 accomplishments

One of Ben Franklin's many accomplishments was bifocal glasses to see near and far.

6 achieve

Wanting to succeed helped Ben achieve, or reach, his goals. This is a statue of Ben.

7 composed

Beethoven is famous for the beautiful music he composed, or wrote.

8 result

When a musician plays the armonica, beautiful music is the result!

471

Background

Benjamin Franklin   Benjamin Franklin was a remarkable man. He composed articles for his own newspaper and for a book he published yearly. Ben also spent great amounts of time helping Americans achieve freedom. Over his lifetime, Ben designed many new things, such as the lightning rod and the odometer. As a result, our lives are improved thanks to Ben's inventions.

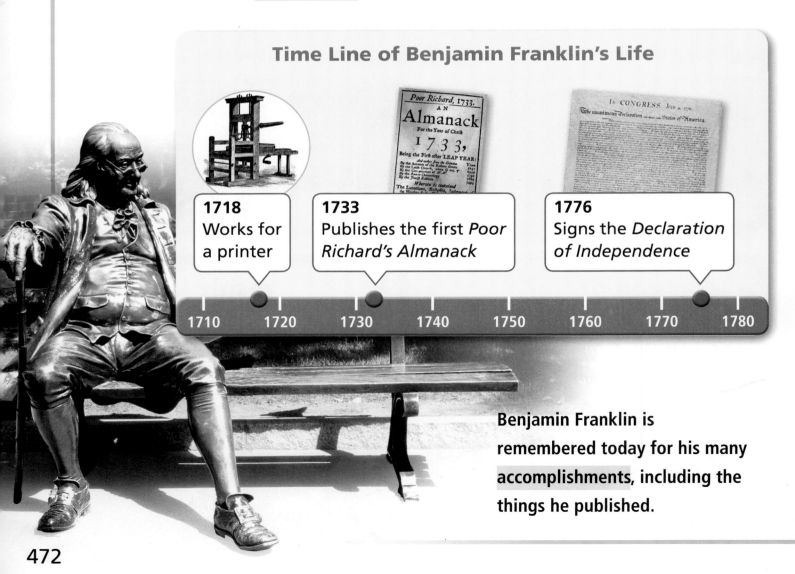

Time Line of Benjamin Franklin's Life

Poor Richard, 1733:
AN
Almanack
For the Year of Chrift
1733,

In CONGRESS, July 4, 1776.
The unanimous Declaration of the thirteen United States of America.

1718
Works for a printer

1733
Publishes the first *Poor Richard's Almanack*

1776
Signs the *Declaration of Independence*

1710 1720 1730 1740 1750 1760 1770 1780

Benjamin Franklin is remembered today for his many accomplishments, including the things he published.

Comprehension

Compare and Contrast

In *Now & Ben*, the author compares things that we have or use now to things that Ben Franklin did or invented. You can use a Venn diagram like this to compare and contrast these details.

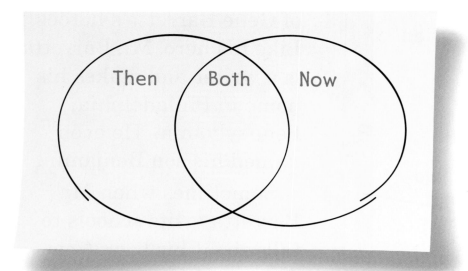

Then   Both   Now

✔ **TARGET STRATEGY** **Visualize**

Use the information in the chart and what you read to visualize how things have changed since Ben Franklin's time. You can draw a picture to help you.

Main Selection

Now & Ben
The Modern Inventions of Benjamin Franklin

✓ TARGET VOCABULARY

inventions
accomplishments
remarkable   achieve
designed   composed
amounts   result

✓ TARGET SKILL

Compare and Contrast Tell how two things are alike or not.

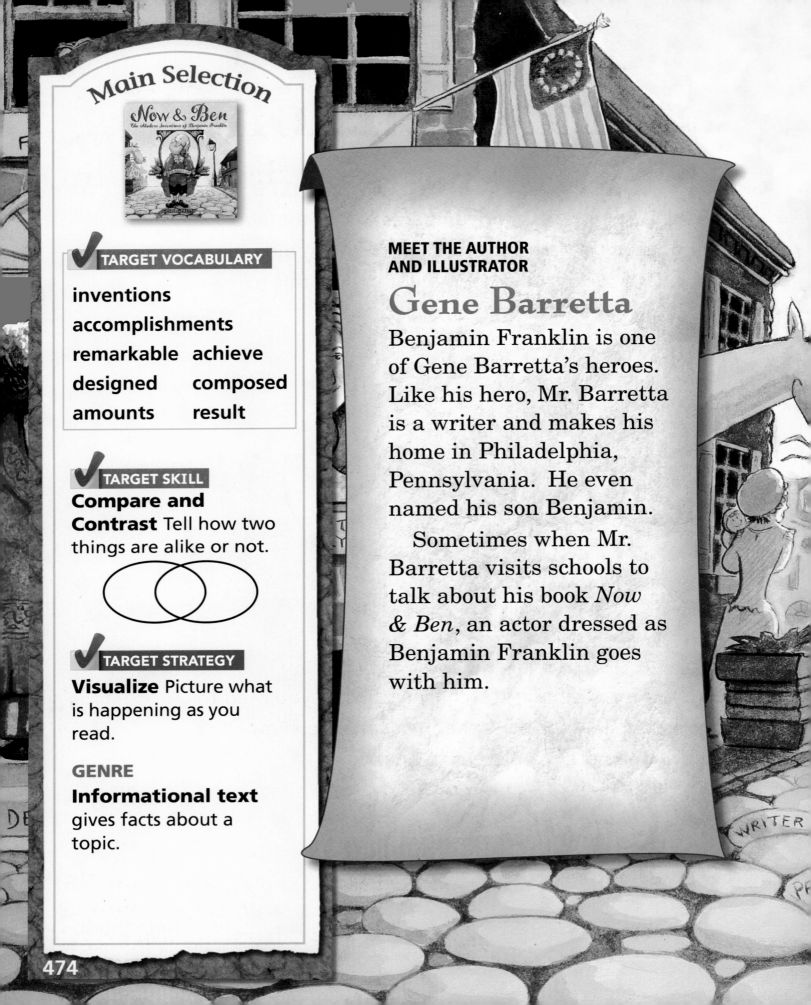

✓ TARGET STRATEGY

Visualize Picture what is happening as you read.

GENRE

Informational text gives facts about a topic.

MEET THE AUTHOR AND ILLUSTRATOR

Gene Barretta

Benjamin Franklin is one of Gene Barretta's heroes. Like his hero, Mr. Barretta is a writer and makes his home in Philadelphia, Pennsylvania. He even named his son Benjamin.

Sometimes when Mr. Barretta visits schools to talk about his book *Now & Ben*, an actor dressed as Benjamin Franklin goes with him.

474

Now & Ben

The Modern Inventions of Ben Franklin

FRANKLIN

written and illustrated by
Gene Barretta

Now and then, we think about Ben.

Dr. Benjamin Franklin, to be precise. And we think about his many inventions—inventions he originated more than two hundred years ago.

It was as if Ben could see into the future. Almost everything he created is still around today. For instance . . .

NOW...

our newspapers are filled with illustrations.

Ben...

was the first to print a political cartoon in America. The cartoon encouraged the American colonies to join together or die like the disconnected snake.

Now...

our world relies on electricity. In the eighteenth century, many people believed that lightning was an act of anger and punishment from God.

Ben...

was one of the scientists who discovered the true nature of electricity and how to use it. He learned that lightning is electricity when he attached a small metal wire to the top of a kite and gathered electricity from a storm cloud.

NOW...

many buildings and homes use lightning rods to protect against lightning strikes.

Ben...

invented the lightning rod and was the first to use it. The pointed iron rod acts like a magnet and grabs an approaching lightning bolt from the sky before it can strike the rooftop. The electricity then travels safely down a long wire into the ground. It prevents fires and keeps dangerous amounts of electricity away from the house.

STOP AND THINK

Author's Craft In what way does the author say that a lightning rod and a magnet seem alike?

NOW...

this gadget goes by many names, such as the Grabber. Everyone has seen one—it's the long stick that helps grab items from out-of-reach places.

Ben...

invented the original device and called it the Long Arm because it worked like a very long arm.

> ✓ **STOP AND THINK**
>
> **Compare and Contrast** What about this invention is the same today as it was when Ben invented it? What has changed?

Now...

swimmers and divers use flippers to move faster through the water.

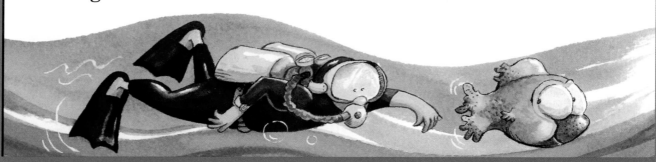

Now...

ships travel across the Gulf Stream to take advantage of the faster current.

Now...

we understand and accept the benefits of vitamin C.

Ben...

invented things even when he was a boy. He was an avid swimmer and built wooden flippers for both his hands and feet.

Ben...

measured, charted, and publicized the Gulf Stream during his eight voyages across the Atlantic Ocean.

Ben...

was an early promoter of eating citrus fruits to help prevent a disease called scurvy.

for a musical interlude.

Ben...

invented the glass armonica. He was able to create music by simply touching his wet fingers to a row of spinning glass bowls. Mozart and Beethoven were so moved by the sounds that they composed for the instrument.

Today, glass armonicas are very rare. You are more likely to find one in a museum than in a music store.

TUNED GLASS BOWLS TURN ON A ROD

WHEEL TURNS THE GLASS BOWLS →

TUNED GLASS BOWLS

FOOT PEDAL MAKES THE WHEEL TURN →

ARMONICA

STOP AND THINK
Visualize How do the details in the description help you hear and picture how the armonica worked and sounded?

Now...

chairs come in all shapes and sizes.

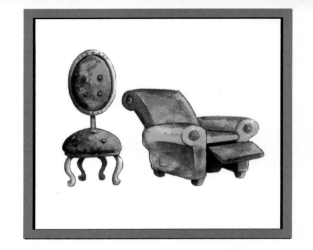

Ben...

designed two chairs that are still very useful. The writing chair combined a desk and chair into one. The library chair was a combination chair and stepladder.

Now...

everyone has seen a rocking chair, but not many have seen Dr. Franklin's rocking chairs.

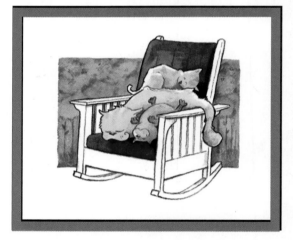

Ben...

invented one rocking chair with a fan on top and one that churned butter.

Now...

every year, we observe daylight saving time, which means we set our clocks ahead one hour in the springtime. As a result, it stays darker longer in the morning when most people are sleeping and stays light longer at the end of the day so we can save more energy. In the fall, we return the clocks to standard time.

Ben...

suggested this idea in one of his essays as a way to save money by burning fewer candles. Farmers could also gain more work time in the evening. Daylight saving time was not officially practiced until World War I, more than a hundred years later.

As for clocks . . .
Ben designed the first clock with a second hand.

487

Now...

every automobile has an odometer to measure the distance it travels.

Ben...

invented the odometer when he was postmaster general so he could measure his postal routes.

NOW...

almost every large community includes a library, a hospital, a post office, a fire department, and a sanitation department.

Ben...

lived in a city that had none of these establishments, so he helped organize the first of each.

NOW... and then, we owe thanks to Ben for his important inventions. But many would agree that his greatest accomplishments came in the form of documents—documents that helped shape the world.

Ben... had a pivotal role in developing America's Constitution, the Treaty of Alliance with France, the Treaty of Peace with England, and the Declaration of Independence. It's remarkable that one man could achieve so much in a lifetime. He has certainly helped to form the modern world. . . .

Will his contributions help to form the future?

Your Turn

Sing Along

A Song for Ben

Think of a song you know, such as "Mary Had a Little Lamb." Work with a small group to change the song's words to tell about Ben Franklin. Include his inventions and why he is famous. Share your song with classmates. SMALL GROUP

Ben Franklin had a great idea
Great idea, great idea
Ben Franklin had a great idea
He made a lightning rod!

Turn and Talk — What a Difference!

With a partner, think about one way that life now is different from life when Ben Franklin was alive. Then discuss how and why your life would be different if you lived during Ben's time. COMPARE AND CONTRAST

Social Studies

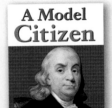

A Model
Citizen

inventions
accomplishments
remarkable achieve
designed composed
amounts result

GENRE
Informational text
gives facts about a topic.
This is a social studies
text.

TEXT FOCUS
A **map** is a drawing of
a town, state, or other
place.

A Model Citizen

Ben Franklin became famous for many reasons. He spent large amounts of his time doing scientific experiments. He designed new inventions. He owned a newspaper and composed many stories for it.

Franklin was a good citizen. He began the first fire company in America. He also started the first public library. As a result, life was better for people.

In 1776, Great Britain had colonies in America. People in the colonies wanted to be free. They fought the Revolutionary War against Britain to become free.

The colonists asked Franklin to help them achieve freedom. He helped Thomas Jefferson write the Declaration of Independence. The thirteen colonies won the war in 1783 and became the United States of America.

The Thirteen Original American Colonies

NEW HAMPSHIRE

MASSACHUSETTS

NEW YORK

RHODE ISLAND
CONNECTICUT

PENNSYLVANIA

NEW JERSEY

DELAWARE

MARYLAND

VIRGINIA

ATLANTIC OCEAN

NORTH CAROLINA

SOUTH CAROLINA

GEORGIA

After the war, Franklin helped to write a plan for the government of the United States. This plan was called the Constitution of the United States.

Ben Franklin had a life full of remarkable accomplishments. He is a model for us all.

This painting shows the signing of the Declaration of Independence. Franklin is standing beside Thomas Jefferson.

Making Connections

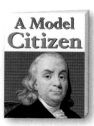

Text to Self

Write a Poem Think about Ben Franklin's inventions and his work for our country when it was new. Write a poem to tell how you feel about his work.

With Ben's fins,
you will swim fast.
In a race,
you will never be last.

Text to Text

Compare Important People Think of another person from real life that you have read about this year. How was this person like Ben Franklin?

Text to World

Connect to Social Studies Tell how Ben Franklin helped his community. What are ways you can help your community? Share your ideas with the class.

Grammar

What Is a Preposition? A **preposition** is a word that shows when, how, or where a noun or pronoun does something. A group of words that begins with a preposition is a **prepositional phrase**.

Prepositions	Prepositional Phrases
with	Ben worked with Thomas Jefferson.
for	He did a lot for people.
in	He lived in the United States.

Turn and Talk **Work with a partner to choose a preposition from the box to complete each sentence. Then tell which words make up the prepositional phrase.**

to   with   in   by

1 Many inventions were made _____ Ben Franklin.

2 Ben lived _____ Philadelphia.

3 He found electricity _____ a kite experiment.

4 He was helpful _____ his friends.

Sentence Fluency In your writing, you can join two sentences that end with the same prepositional phrase. Use **and** between the two subjects.

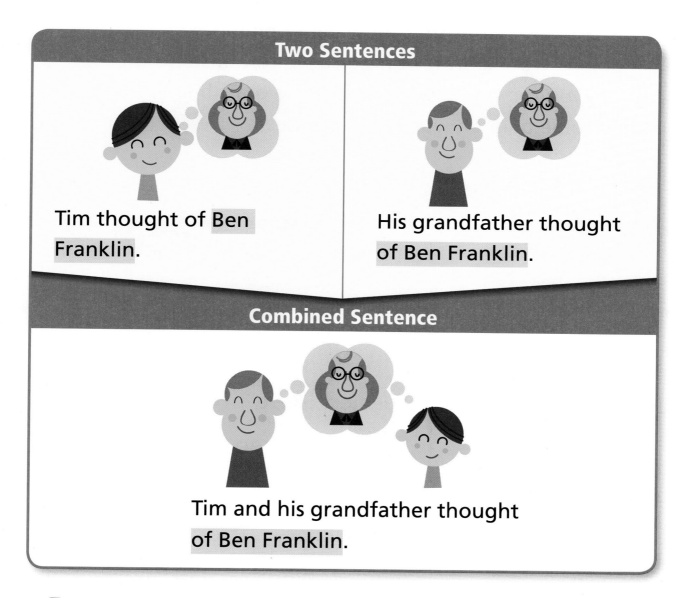

Two Sentences

Tim thought of Ben Franklin.

His grandfather thought of Ben Franklin.

Combined Sentence

Tim and his grandfather thought of Ben Franklin.

Connect Grammar to Writing

When you revise your response essay, combine sentences that end with the same prepositional phrase.

Write to Respond

✅ **Word Choice** When you write a **response to literature**, use words that show your opinion.

Cooper wrote a draft of his essay in response to *Two of Everything*. Later, he revised his draft by adding some opinion words and phrases.

Writing Process Checklist

Prewrite

Draft

▶ **Revise**

✅ **Did I tell things in the order they happen in the story?**

✅ **Did I use opinion words and phrases?**

✅ **Did I sum up my reasons at the end?**

Edit

Publish and Share

Revised Draft

The Haktaks were better off with their special pot. At first it seemed like a ∧terrible problem. But then ~~the problems turned into good things changed.~~ ∧ fortune.

The pot doubled everything for the Haktaks. It doubled their money. When Mr. Haktak put coins in the pot, he got twice the money. ∧ That was wonderful!

The Special Pot Was a Good Thing

by Cooper Jackson

The Haktaks were better off with their special pot. At first it seemed like a terrible problem. But then the problems turned into good fortune.

The pot doubled everything for the Haktaks. It doubled their money. When Mr. Haktak put coins in the pot, he got twice the money. That was wonderful!

The pot gave a second Mr. and Mrs. Haktak. The pot also gave a second home.

> **I added opinion words and phrases to my essay.**

Reading as a Writer

How did the words Cooper added show his opinion? Which opinion words and phrases can you add to your essay?

Read the next two selections. Think about how they are alike and how they are different.

Austin's Famous Flyers

Every summer night, hundreds of people gather around a bridge in Austin. Why? They are there to see bats!

Builders fixed the bridge in 1980. Soon after, bats began moving in by the thousands. At first, many people in Austin were not happy. Many were afraid of the bats.

Then they learned the surprising news. Healthy bats are not dangerous. They are harmless and even helpful. They eat up to 20,000 pounds of insects each night. This includes insects that bite people and insects that eat crops.

Now the bridge is the home of more than a million bats in the summer. People come from all over to see Austin's famous bats.

New Message

Send   Attach   Address   Save

To: Christy

From: Teddy

Subject: My Summer Vacation

Dear Christy,

I am writing to you from Austin. Last night we went to Town Lake. Our parents said we were going to see bats!

As soon as the sun began to set, we saw them. They flew out from under a bridge. They looked like a big, black storm cloud. At first, I felt nervous. Then I learned that the bats do not bother people. I also found out that they eat lots of insects. It was the most amazing thing I have ever seen. I'm now a bat fan!

Your friend,
Teddy

Unit **6** Wrap-Up

A Silly Surprise Cartoon characters show surprise in different ways. They might leap high in the air to show joy or say funny things. Draw a cartoon character getting a surprise birthday gift. Draw a silly action for your cartoon character. Then write a speech balloon.

Listening and Speaking

Show Surprise How do people show surprise? What might a surprised person say? What does a surprised face look like? With a group, take turns acting out the feeling of surprise.

504

Glossary

This glossary can help you find the meanings of some of the words in this book. The meanings given are the meanings of the words as they are used in the book. Sometimes a second meaning is also given.

A

accept
To take what is given: *I accept your gift and would like to give you something too.*

accepted
A form of **accept**: *He accepted the package and waited until he was alone to open it.*

accomplish
To do completely, or carry out: *They accomplish the job by working together.*

accomplishment
A form of **accomplish**: *The concert showed the accomplishments of each musician.*

account
A record of money received or spent: *A savings account helps you keep track of money you put in the bank.*

achieve
To succeed in doing: *Some people achieve a lot by studying on the Internet.*

agree
To have the same idea or opinion: *I agree with you that it is a good day to go swimming.*

agreed
A form of **agree**: *The two friends agreed to meet at the bridge after school.*

amaze
To surprise or to fill with wonder: *The huge redwood trees amaze many visitors.*

amazed

A form of **amaze**: *We were amazed when we saw the first whale.*

amount

Quantity or sum of quantities: *Always measure the **amounts** of juice and milk before you add them to the batter.*

amount

answer

To say, write, or do something in reply: *When you **answer** the questions, write the numbers to go with them.*

answered

A form of **answer**: *Nobody **answered** my call at first, but then I heard a tiny voice.*

assistant

A helper, or one who assists: *He needed an **assistant** to work with the animals.*

astronomy

The study of stars, planets, and other things in the universe: *After reading the small book about **astronomy**, she loved to use the telescope.*

B

blaze

To burn: *The sun may **blaze** too strongly for us to stay at the beach.*

blazed

A form of **blaze**: *Our campfire **blazed** in the darkness and kept us warm all evening.*

blossom

To bloom, or to come into flower: *Fruit trees **blossom** at different times in the spring.*

blossomed

A form of **blossom**: *After the apple tree **blossomed**, we began to watch for tiny apples.*

budget

A plan for how money will be spent: *Our family **budget** includes amounts for food, clothing, and heat.*

C

cage

A space closed around with wire or bars: *Sometimes they shut all their windows and let the bird out of her **cage**.*

cheer

To shout in happiness or in praise: *Everybody will **cheer** and clap when the musicians take their bows.*

cheered

A form of **cheer**: *The crowd **cheered** when the mayor gave her the award.*

chuckle

To laugh quietly: *I sometimes **chuckle** when I think about the silly things we did.*

chuckled

A form of **chuckle**: *They **chuckled** at the comic strip in the newspaper.*

clear

To get rid of or remove: *After the storm, we will **clear** away the branches from the path.*

cleared

A form of **clear**: *When they **cleared** the table after the meal, they planned what to do next.*

compose

To create or make up: *He likes to **compose** songs for the musical each year.*

composed

A form of **compose**: *She **composed** a duet for flute and piano.*

confuse

To mix up: *Sometimes people* **confuse** *twins who look very much alike.*

confused

A form of **confuse**: *The cookies taste salty because he* **confused** *the sugar with the salt.*

contain

To keep inside or hold: *Oranges* **contain** *vitamins and other things that are good for your health.*

contained

A form of **contain**: *The box* **contained** *a new set of pencils.*

contained

control

To direct or be in charge of: *The children learned to* **control** *the hand puppets.*

copy

To make something exactly like an original: *I will* **copy** *this picture in color so you can see the details.*

crop

A plant or plant product that is grown and harvested: *Beans and rice are important* **crops** *in many parts of the world.*

curb

A stone rim along the edge of a sidewalk or road: *Workers are fixing the* **curb** *along this street.*

D

delicious

Tasting or smelling very good: *He made some vegetable soup that was* **delicious**.

depend

To rely on or need for support: *Dogs **depend** on their owners to feed them.*

depended

A form of **depend**: *The group **depended** on her to lead the way out of the forest.*

design

To make a plan for: *We always **design** furniture before we build it.*

designed

A form of **design**: *She **designed** this desk to hold a computer and printer.*

disappoint

To let down hopes or wishes: *I don't want to **disappoint** my parents, so I try to do my best in school.*

disappointed

A form of **disappoint**: *They were **disappointed** that their team did not make the final round.*

discover

To find out, or to find: *It is exciting to **discover** a hidden treasure.*

discovered

A form of **discover**: *When she **discovered** the shiny stones, she showed them to her teacher.*

droop

To bend or hang downward: *When this plant starts to **droop**, you should try adding plant food to the soil.*

droop

drooping

A form of **droop**: *The flower was **drooping** because we left without watering it.*

G5

duplicate

To make an exact copy of: *It is hard to* **duplicate** *a painting with many details.*

duplicated

A form of **duplicate**: *We* **duplicated** *these pictures on a copier.*

dye

Something that gives or adds color to cloth, paper, or other material: *We colored shirts by dipping them in* **dye**.

E

empty

Containing nothing: *The bottle is almost* **empty,** *but you can have the last few sips of water.*

exact

Accurate in every detail: *He hoped to make an* **exact** *copy of the statue.*

exercise

Activity that helps the body: *People and animals need* **exercise** *every day.*

explain

To make clear or give reasons for: *If you* **explain** *what to do, I will try to do it.*

explained

A form of **explain**: *After my father* **explained** *how the camera worked, I began to use it.*

explore

To go into an unfamiliar place to learn about it: *Scientists used special diving gear to* **explore** *the ocean floor.*

explored

A form of **explore**: *Few people had* **explored** *the cave because it was far from the village.*

express

To make known: *Her stories **express** the feelings of the characters very well.*

extra

More than what is usual or needed: *She made an **extra** loaf of bread to give to me.*

F

fail

To be unsuccessful: *We don't want to **fail** to reach the top of the mountain.*

failed

A form of **fail**: *They **failed** to find the missing gloves, but at least they found the scarf.*

final

Coming at the end: *We took a **final** spelling test at the end of the school year.*

finally

At last, after a long while: ***Finally** the long car ride was over.*

fling

Throw hard: *If I **fling** this rock into the water, it might skip over the waves.*

float

To be held up in air or liquid: *The balloon will **float** out of reach if you let go.*

float

flung

A form of **fling**: *She **flung** the ball so hard it went way past home plate and into the bleachers.*

flutter

To flap, beat, or wave rapidly: *Moths **flutter** around the porch light in the evening.*

fluttering

A form of **flutter**: *A hummingbird was **fluttering** around the bright garden flowers.*

force

Power, strength, pressure: *Tree branches broke from the **force** of the wind.*

fortunate

A form of **fortune**: *You are **fortunate** to live in a part of town that was not flooded.*

fortune

The luck that comes to a person: *I had the good **fortune** to win a ticket to the big game.*

fund

A sum of money raised or kept for a certain purpose: *The family has a vacation **fund** that helps them save for summer travel.*

future

A time yet to come: *In the **future** we hope to know more than we know now.*

G

gaze

To look for a long time: *We **gaze** in wonder at the snowy mountains.*

gazing

A form of **gaze**: *They were **gazing** at the pink and purple clouds in the sunset sky.*

grand

Wonderful or important: *He felt **grand** when he marched in the parade.*

grateful

Feeling thankful or showing thanks: *They were so **grateful** for her help that they gave her a gift.*

growl

To make a low, deep, angry sound: *We don't want the bear to growl at us.*

growled

A form of **growl**: *When the wolf growled, she jumped back.*

guard

Someone who protects or watches over: *The guard kept watch all night long.*

guess

To have or offer an idea without all the needed information: *I'll guess that there are about three hundred pennies in the jar.*

guessed

A form of **guess**: *She guessed that the skates would still fit, but she would soon find out.*

H

harm

Injury or damage: *Locusts can cause great harm to crops.*

harmful

A form of **harm**: *Labels on baby toys should tell if they might be harmful.*

heavily

A form of **heavy**: *The snow was falling so heavily that we had to shovel the path again.*

heavy

Weighing a lot, thick, or hard to bear: *This is a heavy box for one person to carry.*

hero

A person who is admired for brave, kind, or important actions: *She is a hero because she helped so many people find safety.*

hurried

A form of **hurry**: *We all **hurried** inside because the rain got very heavy.*

hurry

To act or move quickly: *Sometimes I **hurry** to get to the bus on time.*

I

invention

An original machine, system, or process: *Radios, telephones, and cameras were important **inventions** in the past.*

invention

J

junior

Younger in a family or group: *The **junior** players learned from the senior players.*

K

knot

Tied-together piece of rope or string: *The **knot** was so tight that I had to cut the string.*

L

lean

To slant to one side or to rest on: *You can **lean** your head on my shoulder if you are sleepy.*

leaned

A form of **lean**: *Some people **leaned** against the wall because there were no chairs left.*

lonely

Sad about being alone or far from friends: *He felt **lonely** after his brother left for summer camp.*

O

odd

Unusual or strange: *The car was making an **odd** noise, so we stopped to check.*

orbit

To circle or go around: *Can you name the four largest moons that **orbit** Jupiter?*

ordinary

Common, usual: *This bread you baked tastes better than **ordinary** bread.*

otherwise

If not or if things were different: *I ran fast, because **otherwise** I would have missed the train.*

overlook

To miss seeing, or not notice: *Please don't **overlook** the people who helped make costumes for the play.*

overlooked

A form of **overlook**: *The smallest kitten was **overlooked** at first, but then we found him.*

P

peace

Calm: *If you want some **peace** and quiet, try camping in the wilderness.*

peacefully

A form of **peace**: *The cat dozed **peacefully** in the warm sunshine.*

plan

To decide on what to do: *We **plan** to travel through three states to get there.*

planning

A form of **plan**: *If you are **planning** for the party, be sure to get balloons.*

polite

Having or showing good manners: *Their parents showed them how to be **polite**.*

position

Location, or area that a team player is assigned: *Some players wanted to change their* ***position*** *on the soccer team.*

practice

To do over and over to gain skill: *I* ***practice*** *playing the drums twice a week.*

pretend

To make believe or act as though something is true: *We* ***pretend*** *that we are riding horses when we ride our bikes.*

prize

Something won in a contest: *The* ***prize*** *for the best dancers was a gold trophy.*

prize

promise

To say that one will surely do something: *I* ***promise*** *to write a poem for your birthday.*

promised

A form of **promise**: *She* ***promised*** *to take care of Annie's cat for three days.*

R

receive

To take or get something that is sent or given: *We* ***receive*** *many cards for the holiday every year.*

received

A form of **receive**: *They* ***received*** *a notice about what to recycle and where to put it.*

remarkable

Deserving notice, or outstanding: *The landing on the moon was a* ***remarkable*** *event.*

remove

To take out, take away: *You can **remove** the seeds of the apple after you slice it.*

repair

To fix or mend: *I will **repair** this mower so that I can mow the lawn.*

repair

repeat

To do or say again: *Please **repeat** the directions and I will try to follow them.*

repeated

A form of **repeat**: *The game was so much fun that they **repeated** it the next day.*

result

Something that happens because of something else: *The class mural was a **result** of days of planning and painting.*

roar

To make a loud, deep sound or noise: *Engines **roar** and wheels roll before the planes take off.*

roared

A form of **roar**: *When the lion **roared**, the smaller animals turned and ran.*

S

search

To look over or go through carefully: *We will **search** along the path for the missing gloves.*

sense

Clear reason or good judgment: *It makes **sense** to wear boots in deep snow.*

sensible

A form of **sense**: *Be **sensible** enough to take an extra swimsuit on vacation.*

serious

Thoughtful, important, not joking: *This is a **serious** topic, so please listen carefully.*

seriously

A form of **serious**: *If you take it **seriously**, you should practice the piano every day.*

sharp

Having a fine point or cutting edge: *The knives are **sharp**, so please be careful.*

sharpening

A form of **sharp**: *By **sharpening** the pencil, he could draw very fine lines.*

slippery

Slick or likely to cause slipping: *The rain froze overnight so the streets were **slippery**.*

sore

Painful or feeling hurt: *The shoes were so tight that she had a **sore** toe.*

souvenir

Something kept to recall a special time or place: *I wish that I had more **souvenirs** of the trip.*

souvenir

space

The vast area that includes the solar system, stars, and galaxies: *She became an astronaut because she was always excited about **space**.*

spin

To twist cotton or wool to make yarn or thread: *We learned to spin thread when we studied how families lived long ago.*

spinning

A form of **spin**: *While spinning the yarn, she hummed a tune.*

sprang

A form of **spring**: *The fox sprang out of the tall grass and chased the chipmunk.*

spring

To leap, or move up in a quick motion: *The squirrels spring from the tree to the porch roof.*

sprout

To appear as new growth: *Many plants in the garden sprout in June or July.*

sprouting

A form of **sprout**: *The fields were yellow and green where the corn was sprouting.*

sprouting

stare

To look with a steady, often wide-eyed gaze: *Many people don't like to have someone stare at them.*

staring

A form of **stare**: *Everybody was staring at the huge box and guessing what was inside.*

startle

To cause a sudden movement, as of surprise: *Talking might startle the deer, so be very quiet.*

startled

A form of **startle**: *The ducks were startled by the truck and flew away.*

G15

steer

To guide or direct the course of: *I'm glad that we learned to steer the boat.*

strand

One of the long pieces that are twisted together to make rope or yarn: *The strong rope was made from many strands.*

stream

A body of water that flows in a bed or channel: *A few miles from here, that small trickle of water turns into a flowing stream.*

studied

A form of **study**: *Long ago sailors studied the stars by watching the sky at night.*

study

To try to learn from, or to look closely at: *They study the ant farm to find out how ants work together.*

suspicious

Not trusting, or having doubts: *We were suspicious because last time she tried to fool us.*

suspiciously

A form of **suspicious**: *The mouse watched the snake suspiciously from far off.*

swift

Fast: *A swift rabbit can run away from a hungry fox.*

T

tangle

Snarl or twist: *We tangle the string every time we try to fly our kite.*

tangled

A form of **tangle**: *The kittens tangled the yarn all around our dining room chairs.*

taught

A form of **teach**: *My grandma taught me how to build a birdhouse.*

teach

To give knowledge or lessons: *I can **teach** you how to do that kind of puzzle.*

tear

To pull apart or rip: *I like to **tear** colored paper and make designs.*

tearing

A form of **tear**: *After **tearing** down the old barn, they built a newer, stronger one.*

toss

To throw or pitch: *In this game, you **toss** balls into a basket.*

toss

tossed

A form of **toss**: *The two children **tossed** the beanbag back and forth.*

train

To teach skills or ways to act: *You can **train** your dog to wait quietly.*

training

A form of **train**: *After many weeks of **training**, the team won every game.*

trouble

Something that is difficult, dangerous, or upsetting: *He didn't want to cause **trouble**, so he worked very carefully.*

tumble

To roll or do somersaults: *Mikael likes to **tumble** all the way down that steep hill!*

tumbling

A form of **tumble**: *After **tumbling** across the mat, the gymnast did a split and a cartwheel.*

U

underneath

Beneath, or under: *They ate their picnic lunches* **underneath** *the biggest tree.*

upset

To be disturbed or turned over: *The birds were* **upset** *when the cat climbed toward their nest.*

V

village

A group of houses that make up a community smaller than a town: *There were about fifty people in the whole* **village***.*

W

waterproof

Able to keep water off or out: *For hiking in the rain, you need a raincoat and a* **waterproof** *hat.*

weave

To pass something such as yarn or twigs over and under one another: *The children learned how to* **weave** *a small basket.*

web

Material that connects or ties together: *The spider spun a* **web** *between two branches of the tree.*

webbed

A form of **web**: *Ducks, geese, and penguins have* **webbed** *feet.*

webbed

whistle

Something that makes a high, clear sound when air is blown through it: *The coach blew a **whistle** when he wanted the team to stop and listen.*

wisdom

Being able to judge what is best and right: *People say that you gain **wisdom** after many years of living and making mistakes.*

wonder

To be curious about: *I **wonder** how birds feel when they are flying.*

Y

yarn

Spun wool or nylon for weaving or knitting: *She loved the colors and feel of the **yarn** in the knitting store.*

yarn

Acknowledgments

Main Literature Selections

"Always Be Kind to Animals" from *A Child's Bestiary* by John Gardner. Copyright © 1977 by Boskydell Artists Ltd. Reprinted by permission of Georges Borchardt Inc.

"De Koven" from *Bronzeville Boys and Girls* by Gwendolyn Brooks. Copyright © 1956 by Gwendolyn Brooks Blakely. Reprinted by permission of HarperCollins Publishers.

Dex: The Heart of a Hero by Caralyn Buehner, illustrated by Mark Buehner. Text copyright © 2004 by Caralyn Buehner. Illustrations copyright © 2004 by Mark Buehner. All rights reserved. Reprinted by permission of HarperCollins Publishers.

The Dog that Dug for Dinosaurs by Shirley Raye Redmond, illustrated by Simon Sullivan. Text copyright © 2004 by Shirley Raye Redmond. Illustrations copyright © 2004 by Simon Sullivan. Reprinted by permission of Aladdin Paperbacks, an imprint of Simon & Schuster's Children's Publishing Division. All rights reserved.

"Gloria Who Might Be My Best Friend" from *The Stories Julian Tells* by Ann Cameron. Text copyright © 1981 by Ann Cameron. All rights reserved. Reprinted by permission of Random House Children's Books, a division of Random House, Inc., and Ann Cameron.

The Goat in the Rug by Charles L. Blood and Martin Link, illustrated by Nancy Winslow Parker. Text copyright © 1976 by Charles L. Blood and Martin A. Link. Illustrations copyright © 1976 by Nancy Winslow Parker. Reprinted by permission of Simon & Schuster Books for Young Readers, an Imprint of Simon & Schuster Children's Publishing Division. All rights reserved.

Half-Chicken/Mediopollito by Ala Flor Ada, illustrated by Kim Howard. Text copyright © 1995 by Ala Flor Ada. Illustrations copyright © 1995 by Kim Howard. Reprinted by permission of BookStop Literary Agency, LLC.

Helen Keller by Jane Sutcliffe, illustrated by Elaine Verstraete. Text copyright © 2002 by Jane Sutcliffe. Illustrations copyright © 2002 by Elaine Verstraete. All rights reserved. Reprinted by permission of Carolrhoda Books Inc., a division of Lerner Publishing Group, Inc.

How Groundhog's Garden Grew by Lynne Cherry. Copyright © 2003 by Lynne Cherry. Reprinted by permission of The Blue Sky Press, an imprint of Scholastic Inc.

"Keep a Poem in Your Pocket" from *Something Special* by Beatrice Schenk de Reginers. Text copyright © 1958, 1986 by Beatrice Schenk de Reginers. Reprinted by permission of Marian Reiner, Literary Agent.

Luke Goes to Bat by Rachel Isadora. Copyright © 2005 by Rachel Isadora. Reprinted by permission of G. P. Putnam's Sons, a division of Penguin Young Readers Group, a member of Penguin Group (USA) Inc. All rights reserved.

Mr. Tanen's Tie Trouble written and illustrated by Maryann Cocca-Lefler Text and illustrations copyright © 2003 by Maryann Cocca-Lefler. Adapted by permission of Albert Whitman & Company.

My Name is Gabriela/Me llamo Gabriela by Monica Brown, illustrated by John Parra. Text copyright © 2005 by Monica Brown. Illustrations copyright © by John Para, Vicki Prentice Associates, Inc. NYC. Translations © 2005 by Luna Rising, a division of Cooper Square Publishing. Reprinted by permission of Rowman & Littlefield Publishing Group.

The Mysterious Tadpole written and illustrated by Steven Kellogg. Copyright © 2002 by Steven Kellogg. All rights reserved including the right of reproduction in whole or in part in any form. Reprinted by permission of Dial Books for Young Readers, a member of Penguin's Young Readers Group, a division of Penguin Group (USA) Inc.

Now & Ben: The Modern Inventions of Benjamin Franklin by Gene Barretta. Copyright © 2006 by Gene Barretta. All rights reserved. Reprinted by permission of Henry Holt and Company LLC.

"Old Man Moon" from *In the Woods, In the Meadow, In the Sky* by Aileen Fisher. Copyright © 1965 by Aileen Fisher. Reprinted by permission of the Boulder Public Library Foundation, Inc., c/o Marian Reiner, Literary Agent.

Penguin Chick by Betty Tatham, illustrated by Helen K. Davie. Text copyright © 2002 by Betty Tatham. Illustrations copyright © 2002 by Helen K. Davie. All rights reserved. Reprinted by permission of HarperCollins Children's Books, a division of HarperCollins Publishers.

"The Period" from *On Your Marks: A Package of Punctuation* by Richard Armour. Text copyright © 1969 by Richard Armour. Reprinted by permission of Geoffrey Armour, who controls all rights.

"Quack?" by Mary O'Neill from *What Is That Sound?* Copyright © 1966 by Mary L. O'Neill. Reprinted by permission of Marian Reiner, Literary Agent.

"Share the Adventure" by Patricia and Frederick McKissack. Text copyright © 1993 by Patricia and Frederick McKissak. First appeared as a National Children's Book Week Poem by The Children's Book Council. Reprinted by permission of Curtis Brown, Ltd.

The Signmaker's Assistant written and illustrated by Tedd Arnold. Copyright © 1992 by Tedd Arnold. All rights reserved. Reprinted by permission of Dial Books for Young Readers, a member of Penguin Young Readers Group, a division of Penguin Group (USA), Inc.

"There was a camel..." from *The Sweet and Sour Animal Book* by Langston Hughes. Copyright © 1994 by Ramona Bass and Arnold Rampersad, Administrators of the Estate of Langston Hughes. Reprinted by permission of Oxford University Press and Harold Ober Associates, Inc.

Two of Everything by Lily Toy Hong. Copyright © 1993 by Lily Toy Hong. Adapted by permission of Albert Whitman & Company.

Violet's Music by Angela Johnson, illustrated by Laura Huliska-Beith. Text copyright © 2004 by Angela Johnson. Illustrations copyright © 2004 by Laura Huliska-Beith. All rights reserved. including the right of reproduction in whole or in part in any form. Reprinted by permission of Dial Books for Young Readers, a member of Penguin Young Readers Group, a division of Penguin Group (USA) Inc.

"When I'm An Astronaut" by Bobbi Katz. Copyright © 1995 by Bobbi Katz. Reprinted by permission of the author.

Working in Space by Patricia Whitehouse. Copyright © 2004 by Heinemann Library. Reprinted by permission of Pearson Education Limited.

Credits

Photo Credits
Placement Key: (t) top; (b) bottom; (l) left; (r) right; (c) center; (bg) background; (fg) foreground; (i) inset.
8a (c) Bill Stevenson/Aurora Creative/Getty Images; **10** (tl) Stockbyte Silver/Getty Images; **10** (c) Masterfile (Royalty-Free Div.); **10** (b) Jim Cummins/Getty Images; **11** (tr) Tim Hall/Getty Images; **11** (cr) (c) Blend Images/Alamy; **11** (bl) Robert W. Ginn/Alamy; **11** (br) (c) Ronnie Kaufman/Age Fotostock; **11** (cl) (c) Rolf Bruderer/CORBIS; **12** (b) (c)Michael Newman/Photo Edit; **14** Courtesy Maryann Cocca-Leffler; **36-37** (tl) Stockbyte Silver/Getty Images; **36-37** (bkgd) Stockbyte Silver/Getty Images; **37** (br) Jim West/Alamy; **39** (tr) Stockbyte Silver/Getty Images; **43** Rubberball/Jupiter Images; **44** (tl) (c) Bettmann/CORBIS; **44** (bkgd tl) Siede Preis; **44** (c) Getty Images; **44** (b) Masterfile (Royalty-Free Div.); **45** (tl) (c) Ted Grant/Masterfile; **45** (tr) Tom & Dee Ann McCarthy/CORBIS; **45** (cl) Yellow Dog Productions/Getty Images; **45** (cr) Holly Harris/Getty Images; **45** (bl) Tom & Dee Ann McCarthy/CORBIS; **45** (br) (c) JUPITERIMAGES/PHOTOS.COM/Alamy; **46** (bkgd) (c) David Madison/NewSport/Corbis; **46** (c) (c) CORBIS; **48** Courtesy Penguin Group; **70** (bl) Getty Images; **70** (tl) (c) Bettmann/CORBIS; **70** (bkgd tl) Siede Preis; **70-71** (c) (c) Lake County Museum/CORBIS; **70-71** (bkgd) Siede Preis; **71** (br) (c) Bettmann/CORBIS; **71** (t) (c)1995 PhotoDisc, Inc. All rights reserved. Images (c)1995 CMCD, Inc.; **72** (c) (c) Bettmann/CORBIS; **72** (bkgd) (c) Paul Buck/epa/Corbis; **73** (c) Bettmann/CORBIS; **73** (tr) (c) Bettmann/CORBIS; **73** (bkgd tr) Siede Preis; **77** Masterfile (Royalty-Free Div.); **78** (t) David Buffington/Getty Images; **78** (b) Masterfile (Royalty-Free Div.); **79** (tl) (c) Comstock/Corbis; **79** (tr) (c) JUPITERIMAGES/ Thinkstock/Alamy; **79** (cl) Science Faction/Getty Images; **79** (cr) (c) SW Productions/Brand X/Corbis; **79** (bl) (c) moodboard/Corbis; **79** (br) (c) Bob Sciarrino/Star Ledger/Corbis; **80** (cr) AFP/AFP/Getty Images; **82** Courtesy Full Circle Literary; **109** Digital Vision/Alamy; **110** (t) (c) Jonathan Blair/CORBIS; **110** (b) Mitch York/Getty Images; **111** (tl) (c) Zak Waters/Alamy; **111** (tr) Masterfile (Royalty-Free Div.); **111** (cl) Hola Images; **111** (cr) (c) Jan Tadeusz/Alamy; **111** (bl) (c) Blend Images/Alamy; **111** (br) Benjamin Rondel Photography /Jupiter Images; **112** (cl) (c)1995 PhotoDisc, Inc. All rights reserved. Images provided by (c) 1995 CMCD; **112** (bkgd) (c) Frank Whitney/Brand X/Corbis; **112** (c) (c) Image Farm; **112** (cr) (c) Image Farm; **112** (bkgd b) Panoramic Images/Getty Images; **114** Courtesy Penguin Group; **145** Masterfile (Royalty-Free Div.); **146** (bkgd tl) ASSOCIATED